the OTHER JOURNAL

the OTHER JOURNAL

IDENTITY

An Intersection of Theology and Culture

presented by The Seattle School of Theology & Psychology

Copyright © 2017 *The Other Journal*. All rights reserved. Except for brief quotations in critical publications or reviews, no part of this publication may be reproduced in any manner without prior written permission from the publisher.

Cascade Books
An Imprint of Wipf and Stock Publishers
199 W. 8th Ave., Suite 3
Eugene, OR 97401
www.wipfandstock.com
ISSN 1933-7957
ISBN 13: 978-1-62032-703-6

The Other Journal is based at The Seattle School of Theology & Psychology.

Permissions and Credits
Scripture quotations marked (ESV) are taken from The Holy Bible, English Standard Version (ESV) is adapted from the Revised Standard Version of the Bible, copyright Division of Christian Education of the National Council of the Churches of Christ in the U.S.A. All rights reserved.

Scripture quotations marked (NAB) are taken from the New American Bible, revised edition © 2010, 1991, 1986, 1970 Confraternity of Christian Doctrine, Washington, D.C. and are used by permission of the copyright owner. All Rights Reserved. No part of the New American Bible may be reproduced in any form without permission in writing from the copyright owner.

Scripture quotations marked (NABRE) are taken from the New American Bible, revised edition © 2010, 1991, 1986, 1970 Confraternity of Christian Doctrine, Washington, D.C. and are used by permission of the copyright owner. All Rights Reserved. No part of the New American Bible may be reproduced in any form without permission in writing from the copyright owner.

Scripture quotations taken from the New American Standard Bible® (NASB), Copyright © 1960, 1962, 1963, 1968, 1971, 1972, 1973, 1975, 1977, 1995 by The Lockman Foundation. Used by permission. www.Lockman.org

Scripture quotations marked (NRSV) are taken from New Revised Standard Version Bible, copyright © 1989 National Council of the Churches of Christ in the United States of America. Used by permission. All rights reserved.

Scripture quotations marked RSV are taken from the REVISED STANDARD VERSION (RSV), Grand Rapids: Zondervan, 1971.

On the cover: Lia Chavez, *Light Body*, July 23, 2016, live dance performance by Lia Chavez, Djassi deCosta Johnson, and Troy Ogilvie at Brookhaven Hamlet, NY, commissioned by Isabella Rossellini, presented by Beverly Allan and Nur Elektra El Shami, featuring costumes by Mary Katrantzou, curated by Tali Wertheimer, and photographed and documented by Ira Lippke. Photograph courtesy of Lia Chavez Studio. Image ©Lia Chavez.

THE OTHER JOURNAL

Dan Rhodes :: Editor-in-Chief
Andrew Shutes-David :: Managing Editor
Tom Ryan :: Executive Editor
Chris Keller :: Founding Editor
Zachary Thomas Settle :: Theology Editor
Jeff Appel :: Assistant Theology Editor
Stephanie Berbec :: Assistant Theology Editor
Jessica Coblentz :: Assistant Theology Editor
Brett Potter :: Assistant Theology Editor

Meghan Florian :: Creative Writing Editor
Matthew Shedden :: Praxis Editor
Cabe Matthews :: Assistant Praxis Editor
Julie M. Hamilton :: Art Editor
David Garner :: Associate Editor
Ryan Kelley :: Associate Editor
Lily Greenberg :: Intern
Willow Mindlich :: Intern

EDITORIAL ADVISORY BOARD

Victor Anderson
Daniel Bell
Jason Byassee
William Cavanaugh

Peter Heltzel
Kelly Johnson
Therese Lysaught
Charles Marsh

Charles Mathewes
Michael McBride
Chelle Stearns
Emilie Townes

SUBSCRIPTIONS

The Other Journal (ISSN: 1933-7957) is published about twice a year at the annual rates listed below.
USA Individuals: 2 issues $30.00
USA Institutions: 2 issues $40.00
International Individuals & Institutions: 2 issues $40.00

CONTACT INFORMATION

Send all submissions and queries to submissions@theotherjournal.com or to *The Other Journal* at The Seattle School of Theology & Psychology, 2501 Elliott Avenue, Seattle, WA, 98121

Subscriptions may be ordered online at www.theotherjournal.com/subscriptions.

Subscription e-mail: subscriptions@theotherjournal.com
Advertising e-mail: info@theotherjournal.com
Phone: 206-876-6142
Website: www.theotherjournal.com

Contents

Letter from the Editors ix

1 We were all storm chasers there 1
   Poem by Erin Steinke

2 Strange, Like Pentecost: A Journey for the True Church 3
   Essay by Erick Sierra

3 Autobiographical Memory and the Art of Storytelling and Narrative Identity:
   A Poetics of the Self 10
   Essay by Willow Mindich

4 What Does Where You're From Matter? 19
   Essay by Zen Hess

5 Tit for Tat 27
   Poem by T. M. Lawson

6 Being Pretty 29
   Essay by Katherine James

7 Elena Ferrante's Words Are Good Enough 34
   Essay by Taylor Ross

8 Ta-Nehisi Coates and the Power of Lament 39
   Essay by Zach Czaia

9 Sing More Like a Girl 45
   Essay by Sus Long

10 Performativity and the Flesh:
   The Economy of the Icon in Lia Chavez's *Light Body* 52
   Essay by Julie M. Hamilton

11 We Are Worldless Without One Another:
    An Interview with Judith Butler 64
    Interview by Stephanie Berbec

12 Behind Blue Eyes: Consubstantiality and the Unthinkable 76
    Essay by Russell Johnson

13 Jesus Doesn't Want Me for a Sunbeam:
    Thoughts on Depression, Race, and Theology 82
    Essay by Peter Herman

14 An Unnatural Order 88
    Essay by Ryan Dueck

15 Kinopolitics and the Figure of the Migrant:
    An Interview with Thomas Nail 92
    Interview by Zachary Thomas Settle

16 handiwork 98
    Poem by Oluwatomisin Oredein

17 Street Portraits: Anonymity as Identity
    in the Travel Photography of Mark Wyatt 100
    Photographs by Mark Wyatt

18 Occupied Identity: The Aesthetics of Palestinian Suicide Bombing 107
    Essay by Derek Brown

19 Can't Stop the Feelings: Anger and Identity in Mark 6:17–29 118
    Essay by Angela Parker

20 What's So Holy about Matrimony? A Feminist Theological Reflection 126
    Essay by Kimberly Humphrey

21 Portrait with Eyes Turned Aside 135
    Poem by D. S. Martin

Contributors 137

Pilar Timpane, *Moral Mondays*, Raleigh, NC, 2015, digital photograph.
Courtesy of the artist.

Letter from the Editors

IN 2003, A GROUP of theologically minded graduate students collaborated to form the first online issue of *The Other Journal*. At the time, we observed an uncomfortable alliance between an overtly evangelical president and a religiously driven endorsement of American exceptionalism. We saw that in the wake of 9/11, we were on the verge of two simultaneous (and ultimately protracted) wars in the Middle East. And we believed that if we were to truly understand the moment and challenge the dominant discourse, it was essential to promote theological literacy and Christian ethical discernment.

This is a belief that has continued to guide us over the last fifteen years. Our mission then (and now) was to encourage churches, divinity schools, and Christian leaders to wrestle with real issues in our culture, our theologies, and our community practices. Our hope (then and now) was that this dialogue would help our readers to be sharp interpreters of the culture and that it would shape us toward being thinkers and practitioners who embody and pursue love, justice, and peace.

In 2017, we face a very different cultural/political moment than when the journal first began. And yet, with the election and ascendency of Donald Trump to the presidency, the abrupt shift toward an "America first" mentality, and the emboldening of racism, sexism, environmental assault, and corporate exploitation, our work at *TOJ* now seems more pressing than ever.

As a staff we've felt a pressing need to say *something*, to clearly and unequivocally register our dismay and offer guidance for what to do next. This has been especially true as we sought contributors for our current issue on the theme of identity—we knew that it was vital that we communicate who it is that we are and what we mean to be about. But we have also grappled with how best to offer such a response in this particularly chaotic moment. We have felt the same shock, confusion, and uncertainty that so many others have expressed; and as a journal, we are gravely concerned about the trajectory of a presidential and congressional agenda that appears regressive and destructive with respect to health care, environmental protections, affirmative action policies, and international relations.

Perhaps most disturbing to many of us here at *TOJ*, however, has been the failure of the church to generate and coalesce around sustained movements of social and political alternatives in the face of this threat. We have struggled to understand how so many evangelicals and Catholics could square their own devotion to life with an individual so out of step with the message of the gospel. We have also been perplexed by Christians on the left who have not pushed harder to come together to create communities determined by the collective good, as the theorist Judith Butler encourages us in this issue, rather than the deep sense of individualism that is so characteristic of a society of choice.

Perhaps now more than ever, we desperately need a movement rooted in collective hope and a defiance to empire. To that end, we have a deep theological heritage to draw from, one that has a long and rich tradition of embracing its prophetic voice in the face of oppressive and hegemonic regimes. When German theological institutions signed off on the war efforts of WWI, Karl Barth uttered a defiant theology of refusal, insisting that God stood over and against state politics. Mary Daly revealed and critiqued the ways that patriarchy infused itself in theological discourse, opening up ways of theologizing otherwise. And James Cone, who grew up in the Jim Crow South and experienced the white theological institutions of the United States, asserted the blackness of Jesus as one way to disrupt white supremacy's theological foundations. Christian theology, when at its best, is a discourse of resistance, and this is the history we aim to draw on in our present moment.

Like many of you, we have been moved to action: to march, to contact our representatives in Congress, to donate to causes, and to use our voices. The new administration has signaled its intent to be ruthless (and sloppy) and to circumnavigate traditional institutions and the constraints of law and the Constitution. The need for a movement of resistance—here and now—is real and essential.

But while the Trump presidency is deeply disturbing, we also believe it is time for the church to begin leading a movement that addresses so many of the underlying issues that brought us here in the first place—an abiding faith in neoliberalism that has ushered in a new Gilded Age; a political theory of democracy that sees voting as the primary mode of political engagement; the inability to grapple with or acknowledge institutional racism; and a worship of a debt-driven capitalism that views our bodies as a resource to exploit for profit.

We do not know what the next four years will bring for the world politically, economically, or religiously. Too much is shifting; too much is uncertain. But we do know that Trump has emerged as a symptom of deeper cultural concerns. And as we have tried to do for the last fifteen years, we hope to continue offering you work that is prophetic, resistant, and forceful, work that points the way toward love, justice, and peace.

—Tom Ryan, Jessica Coblentz, Julie M. Hamilton, Brett Potter, Dan Rhodes, Zachary Thomas Settle, Matthew Shedden, and Andrew Shutes-David

1 We were all storm chasers there

by ERIN STEINKE

Nebraska, May 2001

If you don't like the weather
wait twenty minutes, just like that
from sun to tornado, a wild ride—
home base to the edge of town
where the roads flatten into single-lane gravel
as the Kimball county sign flashes by
in lightning that shows we're almost there
almost at its heart
almost got it by the throat
a funnel ready to drop from the telltale
wall cloud, all that potential pressure
and if we drive farther
just a bit faster
we may arrive
see that smoky white shard from the heart of God

stretch to scratch its message in a field—
a hieroglyph in dust and root.

Or the wind may shift
that olive green light
all those sure signs
now tricks and winks
leaving us with bones creaking
in the barometric weight of lost chance.

2 Strange, Like Pentecost:
A Journey for the True Church

by ERICK SIERRA

I WOKE UP IN THE middle of the night to find I'd been sleepwalking, knocking over tables and shattering glass and spilling food across floors, leaving my apartment a wreckage of spiritual hunger. Although it happened in an instant, this coming-to had been decades in the making, for the journey has spanned a much longer distance than these late-night hours or the square footage of my small urban apartment. It has spanned decades and nearly every region of Christianity. By the time I was eighteen, I'd been a Catholic, an inner-city Latin American Pentecostal, and a suburban megachurch evangelical. Later in my twenties, I'd burrow myself in a Southern Baptist church, then in a working-class charismatic church, then in a non-denominational congregation serving an elite university. In my mid-thirties, I'd enter into leadership at a high-brow upper-Manhattan Presbyterian church. Then two summers ago, turning forty, I was received by Holy Chrismation into the Eastern Orthodox Church, anointed of the same batch of oil that graced the Apostles. And now, waking from this long somnambulance of restless seeking, I dart frantic eyes about me trying to gain my bearings: Where am I? How did I get here? What have I been looking for?

My earliest memories of this journey are in the Catholic church of my boyhood, where I served as head altar boy and attended the parish school for eight years. Here,

I experienced God as the roiling of music and the shimmering of liturgy. At the end of Mass, the organist would lose himself in the closing crescendos of his musical score; having fulfilled my altar duties, I'd hurry back into the church to experience the sound amid icon, incense, candle, and glass—an immersive kaleidoscope irradiated with divine Presence.

Driving much of my desire for a heavenly Father was the absence of an earthly father. For twelve years, he had descended into a heroin addiction that shriveled his body and led, finally, to my parents' divorce. He left home when I was ten and disappeared for three years. Then he called one day saying he was back. He had been "delivered" from drugs, he said, "by the hand of the living God."

At first I saw this as just another one of his shenanigans to lure us back, but over time I came to feel that the immanent Presence I'd sensed as a boy had somehow broken through the veil and erupted, fierce and alive, in my father's life. It began remaking him into this man who'd returned to us tall, radiant, ready to love and serve. My parents remarried a year later. In time, my father would go on to become executive director of the drug-rehabilitation program that he himself had completed, Teen Challenge Brooklyn, and to this day he remains the greatest Christian I know.

I fell in love with the church he was attending at the time, a Latin American Pentecostal congregation in Brooklyn. Soon, the mighty force that had seized upon him would start after me. In this environment, my concept of God would transform from ethereal Presence into the winds of disruptive force; as my new spiritual elders put it, I was now being indwelt with the Holy Spirit, *lleno del Espíritu Santo*.

God had given me back my father, so I would dance like David, voice throttling and hands reaching toward Spirit descending. Eventually, I would receive the gifts of the Spirit, particularly the gift of speaking in tongues. As my exercise of these gifts developed, I'd even receive, just a couple of times, a word of prophesy, an intuition concerning a stranger on the subway that would turn out to be true—*but wait... how did you know that? how do you know that about me!* To this day, these experiences are the closest I feel I've ever been to God's reality.

At the time, it never occurred to me to view any of these new religious experiences as materially different from what I'd experienced earlier as an altar boy. I saw my entire journey from Catholicism to Pentecostalism as an unfolding—as if God had been wooing me from behind Catholic imagery in preparation for this new form of relating. Wasn't the God who once filled my mouth with eucharistic grace the same one now filling it with other tongues? *But no!* the people at my church retorted. Catholicism was the "musical chairs" of ritual—at best a distraction, at worst a deception. But I should be thankful, they insisted, that God had led me to a "Full Gospel" church stripped of "man-made tradition" and allowing the Spirit to shine through. So I did as I was told, beating back the Catholic imaginary of my childhood and pressing on to the revelation now entrusted me.

A couple of years later, when I was a senior in high school, my family moved to the Washington DC area and I joined my father in attending a largely white suburban evangelical Bible church that had attracted his attention there. My first impression was that no one spoke in tongues. Why was the Spirit not present? Why were these people not grateful, dancing and raising their hands, exalting God for all he is and has done? I soon began to see what had drawn my dad to this church, though. There was something different at work here. These Christians had a high view of the Bible as God's revelation, and they were living compendiums of scriptural knowledge. What does the Bible say about women in ministry, the proper structure of Christian authority, the relationship between church and state, sex, life, death, even itself? The Bible saturated the community on through to the smallest interactions. As the community enfolded me, they exercised me in the Scriptures. Soon, I became adept at describing the most minute mechanics of salvation—imputation, expiation, justification, substitutionary atonement—with athletic scriptural cross-reference. I was becoming "a man of the Word."

But this led me to wonder why the Catholicism or Pentecostalism of my earlier days hadn't taught me this most essential of spiritual disciplines. My current youth pastor explained that Catholicism had taught me empty ritualism, and Pentecostalism, empty emotionalism, but neither had fed me "the sincere milk of the Word"—the essence of Christianity. Anything that undermines Scripture in this way is a deception that I must cast off if I want to see no longer in part but in full.

But even as I exerted myself in this biblicism, I remained blighted by stubborn mystical proclivities. Despite my best efforts to grow, I kept reverting to a spirituality of the heart, body, intuition. When praying in my bedroom, I'd lift my hands. Why couldn't I just grow forward with gratitude into the true faith now revealed to me? Memories would waft through my prayers. *As a dog returneth to his vomit,* I'd chastise myself. A syllable or two of glossolalia would try to press through. I would hold it back, like an evil thought. An intuition of the Spirit stirring about me, tongues fluttering about the room, shivers of mystic fits. Then I would regain awareness and ask God to pardon this degenerate emotionalism. But then the sonorous vibration of organ pipes would press back into the room, the numinous odor of incense, flashes of the first Christian weeping before her son for me. I'd be back kneeling in my altar boy's pew, enveloped in Presence, at the horizon event of the unspeakable. Then at other times, an inexplicable synesthesia would form of these two Christian pasts: Catholic statues arising from their porcelain platforms and beginning to dance in the aisles, rejoicing in Spanish, ¡Ay *santo, gloria al Señor!*

My youth pastor said I was struggling with "confusion" and medicated me on Bible verses that demonstrated the cessation of Pentecostal effusions millennia ago. I scribbled onto index cards verses warning of the fall of the Papal Church into corruption; I taped them all around my bedroom the better to memorize them. My youth pastor warned, "Wouldn't Satan be willing to lead these poor people into believing they were communing with the Spirit, or with Mary and the saints, if this might lead them away from the light of the Word?"

I wanted a real Christianity, and I undertook the painful amputation this required.

A few years after college, I moved back to New York City to enter a PhD program. I found myself surrounded now by Anglicans, Episcopalians, and Presbyterians at the center of the city's intelligentsia. This was no storefront Pentecostalism in the *barrio*, nor was it your typical suburban evangelicalism.

I came into this new world by way of a small group that was meeting a block from my apartment. It confounded my understandings of what a small group could look like. These people cited T. S. Eliot and Simone Weil in the same thought, the book of Ecclesiastes and Richard Serra together with the Pauline epistles, then all of this finished off with an elegant sip of chartreuse. Where had such an exquisite Christianity come from, and how had I missed it? A Christianity kept a safe distance as much from spastic Puerto Ricans as from suburban evangelicals with unironic mullets. We were liberals, down-with-the-system intellectuals, artists; attuned to nuance, complexity, and culture; VIPs at New York Fashion Week and its after parties. A Christianity of the high mind protected from Papalism, Pentecostalism, and that most accursed of cultural accretions—the Bible-thumping American McChurch. Oh, I'd finally found a place in Christianity to call my home!

We hit the streets one Sunday afternoon to attend art shows. At the end of our day, as we wound our way back in the early evening toward the Midtown subway, I looked up to see the awning of Times Square Church, that Pentecostal bastion where decades earlier my dad had his first encounter with God. This caught me off guard, and I couldn't hide it. I could feel the supernatural energy pulsing through the doorway. *Mi hijo*, I could hear my Pentecostal *pastora* tell me, *el Espíritu Santo will always seek out, no matter how far you run*. It was there again. That Christianity of intuition and the heart. I could feel my chest thrumming to waves of love. The voices of everyone inside shining out like some sort of singing light. *Come on guys; let's worship with them a little. Why not? They're our brothers and sisters too! It'd be at the very least an "interesting" experience of cultural otherness, wouldn't it?*

Inside, I tried to keep my cool, but the hymns pressed tears to my eyes, as if it were the most natural thing for an English professor to be standing, weeping, side by side his fabulous friend aesthetes and hundreds upon hundreds of blacks and Latinos on a Sunday evening. I knew that a lot of the worshippers there had, like my dad, been divinely healed from drug addiction and were rejoicing to be free; I knew that lots of them had, like my dad, regained health, family, purpose, life. *Who can stand in the presence of Power and Love itself*, my dad would ask, *and not weep?*

In a moment, before I could calculate what was happening, I opened my eyes to find through the blur of tears my friends on either side giggling: *Yes, this is Kitschianity at its worst! Thomas Kincaid! Freedom Fries! Oh behold the happy-clappy herd.*

When at the age of thirty-five I met my now wife, she urged me to attend the Divine Liturgy with her at her Eastern Orthodox Church. I told her that I'd explored every region of Christendom—been there, done that, with scars to show—so thank you, but no. But she quietly left a book on the Orthodox faith on my desk one day. After a simple perusing, it provoked me to ask questions I'd never asked before. It soon dawned on me that my knowledge of Christianity had been confined not only to its Western half but its modern-Western quadrant. I knew the library of writings from Martin Luther onward, but what had been the rich texture of Christian theology and practice before Western modernity, and why had I been ignorant of it?

I met with her priest to learn how Christian thought had developed in the early East, radiating out of ancient Greece, up into modern Eastern Europe and Russia and then wrapping around to Alaska. I'd always imagined, I suppose, that the Bible had just dropped out of the sky, ready to read, but why hadn't anyone brought me into dialogue with the living community through whom the Spirit breathed a body of writings that then gained their meaning within the life of that same community? What anterior spiritual understandings led this community—the early Church—to canonize these writings over the many others as testifying to God's work on earth? How did they understand and interpret the writings *they* compiled? I began reading these early Church Fathers and unearthing a deeper Christianity than I'd ever known.

I was forced to revisit some basic beliefs. All those verses I'd memorized at my Bible church about salvation: how had early Christians such as Saint John Chrysostom interpreted them? "God became man," wrote Saint Athanasius, "so that man might become God."[1] In the incarnation, God participated in our earthly life and death in order to assume fallen creation back into himself. For these early Christians, being "saved" had less to do with mental assent to propositions than with participating, in living flesh and blood, in God's divine life through Christ. And the early Church that curated the Bible had also curated rich liturgical practices for our full-self participation in Christ's re-assumption and transfiguration of creation. Liturgy after Liturgy, this more holistic Christianity, hiding for so long in plain sight, disclosed itself.

The Orthodox priest helped me make sense of why I'd endured such heartbreak across the previous decades. Protestants, he explained, had deviated off course from the line of historical continuity that might have given them consistency with original

---

1. Athanasius, *De Incarnatione* 54.3.

Christian thinking and practice. The Western-individualist character of Protestantism insisted that *if I don't like this particular belief, I'll just create another one*, driving its adherents toward perpetual schismatic mania. I stayed up late in the evenings with the priest, who helped me see how this mentality led my former Protestant churches into hermeneutical arrogance. A Protestant will legitimate his own particular denomination "because the Bible says so"; his own particular denomination, if one only read the Bible closely and carefully enough, reveals itself, clearly, to be the true church. Yet ten different Protestants belonging to ten different denominations will claim ten different Bible-centered rationales—chapter and verse and all—to justify their own denomination. Each will insist that, if you just pray sincerely enough and seek God hard enough and renounce your selfish motives deeply enough, you will gain objective clarity into the Scriptures and see the world as *I* do.

Yet, the priest demanded, across hundreds of Protestant denominations, where was that clarity? It was through the Eastern Orthodox Church, he said, that God sought to bring all this demotic squabbling to rest, conferring unity upon minds confused by private interpretations. It was the Protestant compulsion to innovate, to retrofit Scripture to legitimate this innovation, and then to demonize those who innovate differently that imperiled Western Christianity in general and nearly destroyed me in particular.

I would finally become Orthodox, cleaving myself through Chrismation to "the One True Church," "the Very Fullness of the Faith." I would now bring to repose the ontological gnawing keeping me scrambling across decades, pursuing the place where God most fully dwells.

About a year into my new Orthodox life, I struggled with an especially difficult bout of confusion one Sunday morning. Our priest was preaching that heaven would be Orthodox Liturgy just like this, the faithful silently absorbing divine procession forever. Yet when I closed my eyes, I kept seeing a celestial storefront church of working-class Latinos. Shivers of divine eros. Eruption of hands. Shouts of praise. ¡Por siempre tu nombre será exaltado! But they were not alone. Spread out throughout and beyond them was an expanse of Christians somehow doing very different things in unison: crossing themselves at altars, contemplating academic sermons, clapping hands and swaying in choir robes, standing, kneeling, locking hands in expanding rings of dancing—Hebrew cymbals, English boys choirs, African djembe drums, ancient lyres, the worship rock of American millennials. Why couldn't it be, I prayed? Why couldn't the kingdom be the perplexingly beautiful reconciliation of those who respond in love to Christ in whatever way they've had the chance to come in contact with his voice? Saint Basil the Great alongside Billy Graham alongside Pope Francis alongside the thief on the cross—"And heaven will be Liturgy eternal," our priest interrupted, "just as is practiced in the Holy Orthodox Church every Sunday, heretics of the True Faith finally vanquished!"

I tried to press the pleading voices back, press them back and away. I labored to reopen my eyes and resume my forward gaze. I had to focus on Liturgy. I had to prepare for heaven.

Just a few months ago, we attended a church potluck after church one Sunday. As we served ourselves Greek salad and feta burgers, conversation made its way to the Great Schism, that fateful day "when Rome and the West fell into heresy, cutting themselves off from the salvation of the Holy Orthodox Church."

"But"—the words just bubbled out of my mouth—"haven't there been holy Christians in the West from whom we can learn and who will be worshipping in heaven with us? Men and women from across history who have known and loved Christ even from outside of our tradition?"

"Like who?"

And it was then that I realized I'd never really told anyone here. What inspired me to follow Christ in the first place. All this time, I'd remained silent about my greatest argument and hope for a church healed of infighting and terror, remade a unity of parts worshiping in strange, transcendent communion—like the day of Pentecost. This would be the moment.

"Like my dad," I declared. "I've seen the light of Christ in him like in no one else! I lost him to heroin addiction when I was a boy but God gave him back to me a renewed Christian when I was fifteen, and he has served God faithfully all these years!"

"You mean to say: he was *Chrismated* and became *Orthodox*?"

"No, Protestant! Pentecostal!"

Silence. Then the head of the church council, glancing back and forth at the faithful, broke it: *no doubt the father of lies would work miracles for a man freeing him from drugs and whatnot if that might lead him like a puppy down the hole of delusion and darkness, is that not so—*

"Yes, yes, it is so," they responded, looking at one another, and then at him, but not at me.

3 Autobiographical Memory and the Art of Storytelling and Narrative Identity: A Poetics of the Self

by WILLOW MINDICH

According to Greek mythology, the cave of Hypnos can be found by those awaiting death on a poppy-lined mountainside in the underworld. The river Lethe trickles through the soporific cave. The Greeks say that all who sip from the waters of the Lethe will surrender to forgetfulness and be released of all earthly memories. With the lightness of liberation and the soft breath of the damp cave, their supple bodies will fall to the floor of the moonless chamber where they will remain as their souls prepare for reincarnation.

Learning, then, is the rediscovery of the knowledge that lies dormant in the soul. This rediscovery is expressed with the Greek word *anamnesis*, which means to un-forget, remember, or recover the truths that are always already embedded in us. This also explains the derivation of *aletheia*, the Greek word for *truth*, in which the prefix *a* suggests the negation of what follows, *lethe*, or forgetting. Aletheia is the recollection of insights from our past lives, a recollection that draws truth out of concealment. To remember is to rediscover truth.[1]

---

1. For the etymology of *anamnesis*, see Jerry Samet, "The Historical Controversies Surrounding Innateness," in *Stanford Encyclopedia of Philosophy*, https://plato.stanford.edu/archives/fall2008/entries/innateness-history; for the etymology of *aletheia*, see Michael Inwood, *A Heidegger Dictionary* (Malden, MA: Blackwell, 1999), s.v. "aletheia and truth."

These are not the firm and situated empirical truths that some traditions find compelling. These are not truths that can be captured, articulated, discerned, or determined. When we cling to that form of correctness, we risk stifling and enframing the dynamism of the world; we risk mistaking this empirical account for an objective reproduction of the world as it is. And as this happens, something essential is forgotten. Such representational models of thinking reject that the world is constantly developing, and they fail to reconstruct more comprehensive truths that are sensitive to extraordinary and subtle change. Anamnesis encourages us to reimagine a truth that is amenable and responsive to all amendments and modifications, a truth that has not been decided definitively but that instead invites inquiry and adjusts itself to reflect new discoveries.

In this same way, when I speak of remembering, I am speaking of a *poetic* or reconstructive re-remembering and a creative revealing. Martin Heidegger refers to *poiesis* as the artistic gathering of diverse elements and crafting from those elements a human art that resonates deeply with and reveals the essence of the reconstructed materials.[2] It is through this form of poiesis that we are able to rediscover aletheia, and it is through the poetic form of storytelling that we are able to weave together the discrete materials of our lived experience. We pick up the odds and ends of what we remember and what we've forgotten, and we use these to make narratives about ourselves that might deviate from and subvert reality or "what really happened." Yet, through this process, we are able to create more resonant accounts of what has happened to us and of who we are.

RECONSTRUCTION

Because memory is located within a particular kind of philosophy aimed at "capturing" being and making it accessible in the form of logical propositions, memory has been thought of as being primarily representational. It is commonly assumed that when we experience an event, it is consolidated as a mnemonic trace, which is then stored away in the singular repository of the memory, remaining there until some later moment when we are prompted to recall it.

However, in 1932, Sir Frederic Bartlett, the first professor of experimental psychology at the University of Cambridge, challenged this idea when he published *Remembering: A Study in Experimental and Social Psychology*. There, Bartlett argues for a reconstructive approach to memory that problematizes the historically accepted reproductive model. He concludes that memory does not operate as a fixed and rudimentary structure of preserving, stimulating, and reproducing experiences; on the

---

2. Michael Wheeler, "Martin Heidegger," in *Stanford Encyclopedia of Philosophy*, https://plato.stanford.edu/archives/win2016/entries/heidegger/.

contrary, remembrance is a creative process that actively reconstructs events from a developing network of impressions.[3]

This way of understanding memory establishes recollection as a mode of creative composition; to remember is to creatively assemble the past from the perspective of the present. Paul Ricoeur echoes this project philosophically in his 1984 reading of Aristotle's *Poetics*, in which he posits the theory of *emplotment* that explores the distinctly human art of composing narratives. Narrative composition, like the mnemonic process, reconstructs experience to give a sequential order to episodic and isolated events. According to Ricoeur, we poetically reimagine scenarios so that we may lend coherence to our disjointed lives.[4]

Ricoeur's approach suggests that when we remember and identify ourselves, we do so by telling stories. We understand our lives through our evolving narratives. We have narrative identities. However, these stories are constantly being rewritten, and as they change, our identities fluctuate with them. In this line of thought, life stories are the poetic solution to discordance, and remembering is the art form by which we reinterpret our individual experiences and derive meaning from them. Thus, memory has a distinctly personal dimension that evades objective representation and provides us with self-understanding.

DISMEMBERING THE MNEMONIC STOREHOUSE

Demonstrating, once more, the larger tradition of an objective and static approach to being, predominant theories of memory rely on metaphors and analogies of filing cabinets and storehouses in which experiences of past events are crystallized, consolidated, and tucked neatly away in chronological order, to be called upon and summoned for future review or else forgotten. Saint Augustine, for example, evokes a "great field or a spacious palace" where "countless images of all kinds" and "all the thoughts" have been stored away "for safekeeping." Others believe, "the storehouse is [the] place where things are put in the hope that they may be found again when they are wanted exactly as they were when first stored away."[5]

However, recent studies in neuroscience and psychology have discovered that there is no mnemonic storehouse, and thus, there are no pure memories.[6] In fact,

---

3. Bartlett, *Remembering: A Study in Experimental and Social Psychology* (New York, NY: Macmillan, 1932), 200.

4. Ricoeur, *Time and Narrative* (Chicago, IL: University of Chicago Press, 1984).

5. Augustine, *Confessions*, trans. R. S. Pine-Coffin (Middlesex, UK: Penguin, 1961), 214; and Bartlett, *Remembering*, 204.

6. Komáromy, *Figures of Memory: From the Muses to Eighteenth-Century British Aesthetics* (Lewisburg, PA: Bucknell University Press, 2011), 104–05. Reconstructive memory is later pursued by thinkers and psychologists such as Jean Piaget, Edward S. Casey, Jefferson A. Singer and Pavel Baglov, Charles Fernyhough, and Andrea Smorti and Chiara Fioretti.

the reconstructive approach to memory illustrates that the memory is not a passive system of imaging and reviewing the past. Rather, each time we recall an event, we reconstruct it in a new and different way. We recall an event according to our most recent images and rememberings, attitudes and impressions, opinions, understandings, needs, desires, stories, and narratives.

When recollecting an event, we are not transported to some prior point in time as a seven-year-old witnessing our first encounter with lovemaking or death. Instead, we conjure that scene based on our present capacity to interpret what such an event would look like. As stated by Charles Fernyhough, a contemporary psychologist who explores the interstices of literature and memory, remembering can only happen in the present through a "prism of intervening selves."[7] Therefore, in remembering, we ask ourselves how it would feel to be in the midst of such a formative moment.

We imagine what it would feel like to walk beyond the closed door and back out it with shame and misunderstanding. Or, to be standing beside a coffin in the cold wetness of the mid-December rain, several months after the death of a young cousin to whom in the years afterwards you will be compared to and told stories of, and wonder whether you will also be struck from the earth at the age of twenty-three and whether there will be a young child standing there at your funeral in her mother's cloak, who will walk with her soon-to-be step-dad back to the green minivan with her soon-to-be step-sisters with whom she will only speak every third-year. And you will wonder if in the years following your death, the young girl will listen to the recording of the voicemail you left for your mother, panicking, just before the towers collapsed and you died, hoping you could've spoken with her one last time, heard her voice, told her you loved her; and only a couple of years before listening to this tape, that same seven-year-old girl, who is now a young woman, will sit in your bedroom, exactly as you left it, on the night that your father will die of cancer in a room down the hall, and she will look at the photographs on your bedroom wall, recognize herself in them and wonder if you knew her better than she can remember. Sitting there in your bedroom she will find a Magic 8-Ball, the very same Magic 8-Ball that she will give to her now ex-boyfriend to help him make decisions, and on the night that your dad will die she will ask it, "Will my Uncle Bob get to see my cousin again?" to which it will reply, "Undoubtedly," all while sitting at a table fourteen years following your death, contemplating the nature of remembrance and storytelling while writing a reflective essay.

This is how we remember formative events. We do not view them as one would a video reel or an exact replica of that moment frozen in time; rather, we remember definitive moments in narrative form, creating stories from bits of past and present

---

7. Fernyhough, "The Story of the Self," *Guardian*, January 13, 2012, https://www.theguardian.com/lifeandstyle/2012/jan/13/our-memories-tell-our-story.

images that seem relevant and applicable at the moment of remembrance. The story changes with each telling, to each person, for new information is often gleaned, and as this happens, the identity shifts, new understandings emerge, and the elements that comprise the story are displaced and replaced.

THE MNEMONIC SCHEMA

For Bartlett, past experiences are constituents of an evolving framework, or schema, into which active impulses are filtered and modified, and patterns of remembering and understanding are developed.[8] Whenever a mnemonic entity enters the frame, whenever something new is remembered, the experience is molded by its relationship to other memories, and other memories are modified by their relationship to the incoming impulse. There is a constant interplay of new and former experiences. The memory system constantly rearranges itself, and as it does so, the memories themselves are reassembled. Because of this, an event is uniquely re-created with each recollection. This living mnemonic schema also weaves together emotional and intellectual information, assembling stories and narratives while reinterpreting our pasts from our situatedness in the present.

Zsolt Komáromy suggests that we would not be able to define all of the unconscious and internal as well as the outer, more observable conditions of our past experiences that relate us to the world. Memory then has the freedom to choose "among these relations, building out of them a new experience, always differing in some ways from the original it re-creates." This does not suggest that "remembering would be free of all external factors determining it." On the contrary:

> The autonomy of memory depends precisely on these determining factors: the more such there are, paradoxically, the greater is memory's autonomy, since the more relations to the world there are involved in a recollection, the greater the density of experiencing embraced by memory, the greater latitude there is for selection, for shaping, for the freedom of construction.[9]

With each incoming impulse there is a greater opportunity for creative composition. The larger the developing network of memories and experiences (i.e., instincts, impulses and desires, interests and ideals, knowledge, information, and inklings), the more relationships there are to be delineated and the more possibilities there are to compose personal narratives. Memory, then, is not a reduplicative system of reproducing the past; rather, memory is a complex and developing system that creates scaffolds of meaning while poetically reconstructing the past.

8. Bartlett, *Remembering*, 200–15.
9. Komáromy, *Figures of Memory*, 104–05.

I do not remember the death of my cousin as a singular or untouched reproduction of the day itself. When I recall that day, I do so with all of the associations I currently have. I actively reconstruct the image of being a young girl, imagining what it would feel like to be in that body. In doing so, I impose my current understandings of death, family, children, and many more emotions and sentiments that I harbor about the effect of that day and what it represents to each of the members of my family. I take these fragments of experience—the image of a cemetery, the rain, the mourners, the green minivan, the photographs in my cousin's room, the Magic 8-Ball, the conversations with my grandmother—and with them, I build up a scene. I build up a world. I build up a story, and within the image that I have now conjured of the funeral stands each of these elements, wound up inextricably, if only momentarily, with the memory of my cousin's death.

The reconstructive approach brings "memory into line with imagining." From this perspective, "memory is endlessly creative."[10] It is dynamic and fluid. Memories communicate with our desires and mimic the movement of our interests and opinions. As our understandings evolve, our memories do too. As Bartlett states, "If, then, we have to treat the traces as somehow living and carried along with these active factors of 'schematic' organization, it is no wonder that they display invention, condensation, elaboration, simplification and all other alterations."[11] Similarly, our memories reflect our present understanding of the world and our own lived experience; we are known to assemble stories of the past to substantiate our beliefs. For these reasons, "memory [is] imprecise if viewed as a mechanism accurately reproducing discretely stored items of data."[12] Memory is not an empirical repository of historically irrefutable evidence but an art by which we actively reconstruct, dismember, and re-remember our pasts.

EMPLOTMENT AND THE POETICS OF STORYTELLING

Although the term *poetry* descends from poiesis, poiesis does not refer to poetry alone. Instead, the ancient Greeks used the word more generally to describe an art form that is an active doing, making, and creating. It is a meeting point of the self and the world that transforms natural material and uninterpreted experience into something entirely new and intensely personal.

In the *Poetics*, Aristotle speaks of two entities that together produce poiesis. The first concept is called *muthos*, which Ricoeur translates as *emplotment*. This is a process of unifying disconnected events, organizing experiences, and composing

---

10. Bartlett, *Remembering*, 214; and Fernyhough, "The Story of the Self."
11. Bartlett, *Remembering*, 212.
12. Komáromy, *Figures of Memory*, 105.

narratives. When we participate in emplotment, we situate discordant events into the narrative arc of story.

The second entity that constitutes poiesis is a concept referred to as mimetic activity or, in Greek, *mimesis*. Mimesis is often translated as mimicry or imitation; however, Ricoeur insists that we resist affiliating this concept with mere reproduction. Instead, we must understand mimetic activity "in the dynamic sense of making a representation, of a transposition into representative works." That is, we must understand it as an artistic and expressive depiction of an event that alters and transforms the original.[13]

Ricoeur argues that human beings instinctually understand through narrative explanation. As a result, we have a narrative understanding of the world. We actively produce "plots in relation to every sort of static structure, anachronological paradigm, [and] temporal invariant."[14] We fathom our own lives by composing plots that represent them.

For instance, when I am prompted or inclined to explain myself and proclaim who I am and why I am Willow, I do so by telling a story. I could make use of a few adjectives, "curious, quiet, concerned," but these traits could belong to anyone. So, if I would like to share with you the essence of what I feel—the core of emotion and understanding that sits in my upper chest cavity, that has been slowly and progressively developed through pain, passion and regret, and countless excruciating and seemingly insignificant moments of being—I will tell you a story. The story of who I am. I am not an impersonal amalgamation of events but the recipient of experience; I am the subject that is wrought with anxiety and determined to understand it. My narrative makes my life meaningful. It is the story that I tell that relates who I am and how I experience the world. The truth of who I am emerges with my story.

As demonstrated here, humans make sense of experience in narrative form. Consequently, if narratives are composed through muthos (emplotment) and mimesis (mimetic activity), and narratives produce meaning, then muthos and mimesis are the processes of making meaning. And, if poiesis is the craft of composing stories that is mediated through muthos and mimesis, then poiesis is the art form by which humans understand their lives and make them meaningful. As such, narratives are the mythopoetic result of the primal act of narratively understanding who we are.

Ricoeur illustrates how we draw from the aggregate of isolated and incongruent events and thread them together to posit a theory of how we have come to be. Each element represents a probable cause for the next, which makes the story whole and complete. Aristotle suggests that a thing is whole when it has a beginning, a middle, and an end. However, "it is only in virtue of poetic composition that something

---

13. Ibid., 33.
14. Ibid.

counts as a beginning, middle, or end." Further, what constitutes "the beginning is not the absence of some antecedent but the absence of necessity" in the created sequence of events; "as for the end, it is indeed what comes after something else, but 'either as its necessary sequel or as its usual [and hence probable] sequel.'"[15] There is no beginning, middle, and end in the lived experience. As poets and narrators, we create them. Thus, "to make up a plot is already to make the intelligible spring from the accidental, the universal from the singular, the necessary or the probable from the episodic."[16] To make a plot is to create a meaningful sequence of chance events.

When emulating and representing actions and organizing events, we find pleasure in comprehending the incomprehensible, making conclusions from the unfinished, and recognizing the form of that which is often jumbled and without order. In doing so, it is possible that "this pleasure of recognition . . . presupposes . . . a prospective concept of truth, according to which to invent is to rediscover."[17] Therefore, in the process of identifying compatible elements of experience and delineating relations between them, self-truths are revealed and the inner-workings of the mind are given form.

Thus, when we speak of mimesis, the operation by which we creatively emulate experience:

> We must not understand by the word some redoubling of presence, as we could still do for Platonic mimesis but rather the break that opens the space for fiction. Artisans who work with words produce not things but quasi-things; they invent the as-if.[18]

Each time a plot is constructed and story is told a possible truth is brought forth. When we speak of the break, the rupture, the fracture, and the fragments, we speak of the distance, the space, and the clearance that makes room for prospective connections to be drawn and redrawn, for stories to be written and rewritten and for possibilities to be disclosed and revealed. As storytellers and narrators, we poetically compose our own malleable truths, challenge them, deny them, and create them anew.

NARRATIVE IDENTITY AND A POETICS OF THE SELF

According to the narrative view of personal identity, as theorized by thinkers such as Marya Schectman and Alasdair MacIntyre,[19] identity is constructed through the

15. Ricoeur, *Time and Narrative*, 38.
16. Ibid., 41.
17. Ibid., 42.
18. Ibid., 45.
19. David Shoemaker, "Personal Identity and Ethics," in *Stanford Encyclopedia of Philosophy*, https://

narrative composition of autobiographical memory. That is, we piece together our identities through the narration of a life story. However, these constructed identities are not like that of a physical entity with a fixed form. Rather, "these identities are mobile . . . narrative identity takes part in the story's movement."[20] Consequently, if our identities are formed through the emplotment of autobiographical memories, and autobiographical memories are in a state of possible flux that is mediated through the scaffolding system of interchangeable fragments of experience, then identity, too, is a poetic construction. We compose stories to understand who we are and the world that we live in. We are the myths we create, the stories we tell, the narratives we compose, and the truths we bring forth. We poetically create the self. We are poetic creations; we are mythopoetic, auto-poetic beings. Through anamnesis we rediscover the self by poetically re-membering who we are.

In this vein, we ought to reconsider what we mean by truth, and the mnemonic system that creatively partakes in restructuring the self helps us to revisit ancient models of knowledge and revise them. In fact, the reconstructive approach to memory and the poetics of the self provide an avenue by which we can rethink the infallibility of representational systems of knowledge and notions of protected and unalterable truths. It is possible that many of the truths that we define ourselves by are more malleable and imperfect than we are willing to concede. And if we welcome the possibility of a dynamic and comprehensive truth that is sensitive to change and compatible with flux, we might discover that there are further delineations to be made and connections to be drawn and thus more opportunities for our narratives of the world and of others to be poetically reimagined. Through anamnesis, we rediscover truth by re-membering and redefining our relationship to it.

plato.stanford.edu/archives/win2016/entries/identity-ethics/.
20. Ibid.

4 What Does Where You're From Matter?

by ZEN HESS

ELON MUSK, THE PROGENITOR of SpaceX and other tech companies, says humans have two options. Option one: we can find our way to Mars, inhabit it, and survive. Or option two: we stay on Earth and face an extinction event.[1] This, I suspect, is an effective way to raise money for his space project. Americans are enthralled by the prospect of world-ending disaster and the hope of escaping it. There is a reason that movies like *Mad Max* and *Avatar* gross hundreds of millions of dollars at the box office. Part of what draws us to these movies is the action and drama, but the apocalyptic scenarios also get inside our heads and interrogate us. They ask us about who we are and how we got that way. And they give us a glimpse of how the devastation of a place leads to a deeply wounded identity.

Take *Interstellar*, for instance. After another century of undeterred growth and greed, the Earth's land is stripped of its nutrients and crops begin to suffer from blight. There is global hunger. Our protagonist Cooper, played by Matthew McConaughey, was trained as an engineer but has, out of necessity, become a farmer. He is described as "born forty years too early or forty years too late." This suggests a struggle to make sense of his identity in an unsettled place. He laments that "we used to look up and wonder at our place in the stars. Now we just look down and worry about our place in the dirt," and in the wake of the film, this probing sense of identity presses on viewers, asking us where we are, where we belong, and what we should we be doing. Are we

1. Alex Davies, "Elon Musk: We Need to Leave Earth or Risk Extinction," *Business Insider*, May 30, 2013, http://www.businessinsider.com/elon-musk-leave-earth-or-risk-extinction-2013-5.

primarily, as Cooper thinks, pioneers and explorers tasked with discovery? Or are we caretakers who are responsible for tending to the Earth? These questions are heavy with significance and, I believe, they are already echoing in our minds, waiting to be amplified by movies like *Interstellar*.[2]

So where are *you* from? On the surface, this is not a complex question. It is often the first question asked of us by a stranger. Most people will answer by naming the city, town, or state in which they were raised. I, for example, might say Huntington, Indiana. But in this answer, we discover just how complex the question actually is, because Huntington is not a simple answer. Huntington is a place saturated in a particular history and culture, and this is true of all places. When I say Huntington, I am not simply giving a geographical position; I am giving a social context. I am giving a set of parameters for beginning to understand who I am, or at least who I might be. Said differently, our identity is always tied up with a place.

WHAT'S IN A PLACE?

The idea of place has become more complicated in the last several generations as telephones and the Internet have made it possible to be in several places at once. It sometimes seems that people are more invested in a social media place, such as a Facebook community, than they are in their nontechnological places.

Other social phenomena have also complicated our understanding of place. Fast food is one place to start. Michael Pollan, a professor and author, estimates that nearly 20 percent of Americans' meals are eaten in their cars.[3] Where the table was once a place of respite, a moment of familial unity to interrupt the busyness of the day, it now collects dust, unopened junk mail, and other items too troublesome to put away in a hurry. We are now more transient than ever, in both physical and technological places, and our transience inevitably affects our identity or, at the very least, our ability to know our identity.

Wendell Berry observed our transience over forty years ago. He suggests that it stems from the loss of a healthy farming culture in America, a loss that was exacerbated by the exodus of farmers to the city.[4] The culture of a *healthy* farming

---

2. I am indebted to Norman Wirzba for helping me realize the significance of these movies in relation to understanding the significance of place. See especially "On Not Knowing Where or Who We Are," in *From Nature to Creation: A Christian Vision for Understanding and Loving Our World* (Grand Rapids, MI: Baker, 2015).

3. Pollan, *The Omnivore's Dilemma: A Natural History of Four Meals* (New York, NY: Penguin, 2006), 110.

4. In the 1920s, about 30 percent of the American population were farmers; in 1988, that number had fallen to about 2 percent ("Farm Population Lowest Since 1850s," *New York Times,* July 20, 1988, http://www.nytimes.com/1988/07/20/us/farm-population-lowest-since-1850-s.html). Another relevant statistic to consider is that "the total number of farms has declined from 6.5 million in 1935

community is complex, Berry says, and displays traits such as "communal order of memory, insight, value, work, conviviality, reverence, aspiration." Within this culture a certain kind of mind is cultivated—a mind that "has learned the disciplines necessary to go ahead on his own, as required by economic obligation, loyalty to his place, pride in his work. His workdays require the use of long experience and practiced judgment, for the failures which he knows that he will suffer."[5] If the mind of the farmer was lost upon arriving in the city, then what has replaced it?

According to Berry, the mind and character of the responsible farmer is mostly being replaced by "the knowledge of some fragmentary task that may be learned by rote in a little while." Put another way, the mind of the farmer has been replaced by the mind of industry.[6] This industrial mind is specialized or, in Berry's words, fragmented. That is, the industrial mind expects people to do only one specific job. In industrial farming, specialization means that a farm will raise only one crop or one animal. In industrial manufacturing, specialization means that a factory worker will work only within one area of the production line. One could argue that specialization enables people to become masters of their craft, but the cost of specialization is very high. It encourages a kind of tunnel vision in which the connections between systems are overlooked. For example, an economic specialist in a place like Flint, Michigan, might think it makes good sense to switch people's water source to the Flint River because that specialist is primarily taught to consider the financial implications of decisions. A culture taught to think in terms of specialization will fail to see how its economic actions might affect the social, political, technological, or environmental lives of others around the world or, in the case of Flint, those downstream. In this way, the industrial mind is simplified, for it fails to attend to the complexity of interdependent systems.

The second simplification of the industrial mind is its transience: the industrial mind assumes no meaningful connection to its place. We in the United States are painfully reminded of this every time a factory shutters its local production so that it can employ cheaper labor elsewhere. The industrial mind has its eye on efficiency and expansion, place being only a passing concern. We can again think of fast food: how

to 2.05 million in 1997" (Frederick Kirschenmann, "The Current State of Agriculture," in *The Essential Agrarian Reader: The Future of Culture, Community, and the Land,* ed. Norman Wirzba, [Berkeley, CA: Counterpoint, 2003], 102).

5. Berry, *The Unsettling of America: Culture and Agriculture* (San Francisco, CA: Sierra Club Books, 1996), 43–44.

6. Ibid., 45. Like any cultural shift, this replacement takes a great deal of time. It does not defeat Berry's assessment if we see the best parts of a healthy farming community within certain industrial settings—I certainly know many people who, while working industrial jobs and conforming to the industrial mind, maintain the cultural complexity Berry here ascribes to the farmer. What is troubling, however, is that this cultural shift can, and may already have, reached a point of irreversibility, a point at which we can no longer expect what remains of the healthy farming culture to continue on in any meaningful sense.

often have we ordered a burger from a drive-through lane, just off the highway, and then merged back into traffic without having a clue about where we are in the world? Most of us never know the farmer, the state, or even the region in which the cow we're eating was raised. That's because in fast food—or industrialized food—place is irrelevant.

And here, when the mind of the farmer is replaced by the industrial mind, we see evidence of the simplification of character. Norman Wirzba, in his book *From Nature to Creation*, elaborates on this point:

> To know how to live presupposes that we know who we are and where we are. For example, to be dressed in an athletic uniform and in a gym means that I am going to play a game of some sort. What I am to do follows from where I understand myself to be located (an athletic facility) and who I perceive myself to be (an athlete). But what if it is impossible for me to know that the place I am in is a gym and that I am an athlete, which places and calls me into a particular kind of role?[7]

The industrial mind, with its transience, creates in us a sort of ethical amnesia, a confounded character. When living according to the industrial mind, we feel no sense of connection to a place, so we forget how it is that we ought to live in that place. Without a rooted sense of place, we are "basically passive, occupying a provisional, endlessly changeable identity."[8] Unlike the farmer who knows her place, who feels it in her bones, the industrial mind is transient and confused about who it is or what it ought to be doing.

WHERE DO WE BELONG?

We Christians are as prone to accept the industrial mind, and the simplification of mind and character that comes with it, as anyone else. We struggle to understand our own place.

We must not be too harsh on ourselves—after all, our Savior said "The Son of Man has nowhere to lay his head" (Luke 9:58 NASB)—and yet Christians do have a heritage of belonging to places. We are a people of Eden, a place that we were to tend and care for, a place that clearly identified us as creatures of a God who wanted us to flourish with the rest of creation. We are a people of Israel, a place that embodied in its fruitfulness God's faithfulness to the people God liberated from Egypt. And we are a people of the new earth, a people called to look forward to the coming restoration of all things—the making new of all things—when Christ returns to establish a

---

7. Wirzba, *From Nature to Creation*, 10.
8. Ibid., 9.

permanently redeemed world. In all these things, we must confess that Christians are a people tightly bound to and deeply in need of a place.

It should go without saying, then, that I believe that genuine Christian living must deeply consider the meaning of place. We must attempt what Berry calls "the reverse movement"; we must counteract the simplification of mind and character by pursuing the hard work of "establishing complex local cultures with strong communal memories and traditions of care."[9] I am not now imagining something like the Moral Majority, which sought to reverse certain cultural trends, starting with desegregation, through political power and legislation. That effort is wholly born from the industrial mind, for it assumes that culture can be imposed upon a people through the creation of new laws, as if culture could be manufactured. It does not consider that culture is enlivened over time, brewing in the exchanges of people who care about their shared life. Instead, I am envisioning a renewed emphasis on *practices* within our church communities that produce the kind of culture that is appropriate to our place.

Is it good and right that pastors are sometimes projected onto screens instead of being in the place where the people are gathered? Is it good and right that we do not know or wish to know the people with whom we worship? How can we build the kind of community that Berry advocates? How can we find our place? We must find practices that raise questions about transience in our churches.

We have a possible answer, I think, in Paul's first letter to the Corinthians. In that letter, he is adamant that the church's practice of eating together is significant. When the Corinthians eat, Paul says, they should "let no one seek his own *good*, but that of his neighbor" (1 Cor. 10:24, italics mine). Thus, Paul explains that if eating some food causes our neighbor to stumble, then we'd better not eat it. In other words, we are to be intentional with how we eat. Our identity is not located in our ability to decide for ourselves, as the transient American culture insists, but in our place at a table full of people with whom we share our life. Later on, when the Corinthians are gathering for the Lord's Supper, Paul reprimands their lack of intention:

> But in giving this instruction, I do not praise you, because you come together not for the better but for the worse. For, in the first place, when you come together as a church, I hear that divisions exist among you; and in part I believe it. For there must also be factions among you, so that those who are approved may become evident among you. Therefore when you meet together, it is not to eat the Lord's Supper, for in eating each one takes his own supper first; and one is hungry and another is drunk. What! Do you not have houses in which to eat and drink? Or do you despise the church of God and shame those who have nothing? What shall I say to you? Shall I praise you? In this I will not praise you (1 Cor. 11:17–22).

---

9. Berry, *Unsettling*, 45.

Our identity, Paul suggests, is not found in the things that divide us. Our identity is not found in our wealth or our power, those traits that might allow us to eat and drink to the shame of the poor among us. Instead, our identity is found in our place at the table alongside the people of God and before our Lord whom we remember there. By continuing to eat as if our economic, political, or social position actually mattered, we are "despising the church" and "shaming those who have nothing." We are to govern our table manners, according to Paul, in a way that evidences our understanding of and commitment to where we are and whom we are with. In other words, if we are at the Lord's table, then we shouldn't be acting like we are at a business dinner.

Paul tells us that we meet God in Communion; he shows how Communion invites us to engage in our complex local culture and traditions of care. When we take Communion, we are instructed to "judge the body rightly" or to be "disciplined by the Lord so that we will not be condemned along with the world" (1 Cor. 11:27–32). In eating together, we see those among us who "have nothing" and offer them food, rather than turning them into statistics. In taking Communion, we are drawn to a place that gives us identity, a place that gives us a people, responsibility, and a sense of meaning. Moreover, by taking Communion, we are rooted in the body of Christ, which is not a spiritual concept but a living reality. By taking Communion, we are forced to acknowledge the real people, the real place, and the real food that shape how we live in the world. And thus, when we choose not to participate in Communion regularly, we become disconnected from the responsibility of engaging in our community, of giving ourselves to the community in vulnerability and trust.

But we also need a communion practice that resists individualism and transience. We need a communion practice that looks more like community and less like a fast-food meal in the car. I am speaking here primarily to my evangelical sisters and brothers. In the evangelical churches I have attended, Communion tends to consist of each individual helping his or herself to a tiny cup and a tiny wafer. This act, it seems, is only a sacred moment between the congregant and God—there are no interactions with other members of the community. For those of us working in the industrial mindset, such a practice seems normal. What does it matter how we get the task done, as long as it gets done? Why is it important to engage with others if Communion is primarily about me? Matters such as conviviality, a fundamental aspect of biblical Communion, are lost in this method of taking in Communion.

In contrast, most other traditions have ministers of Communion who speak to each individual, make eye contact, and serve the bread and cup. In this way, the practice of Communion resists transience, especially the transience inherent in projecting a pastor onto a screen. A person on a screen can hardly know the complex makeup of the congregation gathered in front of the screen. Only a person present within the congregation can understand that community. Those who offer Communion do not offer only the bread and wine of Communion but also a hand of fellowship that says "We are in this together." Unless we mean to mimic the loneliness of the transient, industrial mind, we must embody our Communion with interaction and intention.

And if we want to be *really* intentional with how we practice Communion, we could go one step farther. We could make our own bread out of ingredients purchased from local farmers. We could work it together. We could bake it together. We could challenge the individualism that causes our deepest divisions by making the practice of Communion fully communal. Communion would bind us to our place by supporting local agriculture and to one another by the act of making, giving, and receiving. Practicing Communion in this way models an alternative way of life for those in the church, a way that challenges the anonymity and specialization so deeply embedded in Western culture. Communion done in this way could become for us an act of participatory discipleship.

Writing about the value of buying from local farmers, Bill McKibben says,

> A tomato from the small farmer at the end of your suburban road takes less fuel to transport, and a tomato from the farmer at the end of your suburban road tastes better. But it's more than that—it's better because it comes from a . . . farmer down at the end of your suburban road. Getting that tomato requires you to live with a stronger sense of community in mind . . . requires that you shed a certain amount of your hyper-individualism with a certain amount of neighborliness.[10]

McKibben is not just theorizing. People have "ten times as many conversations at farmer's markets as they do at supermarkets." By buying locally, "you go from being a mere consumer," McKibben concludes, "to being a participant" in the community.[11] Imagine if we practiced Communion in a way that urged us to be neighborly or to meet our neighbors! Of course, practicing Communion as an act of memory is a good start. We must not forget, however, that we are remembering the Christ incarnate in a way that should ultimately transform our behaviors, compelling us to be neighborly. We are not mere consumers; we are participants. Practicing Communion as a communal act, a neighborly act, helps us establish ourselves in our place and, so, helps us understand where we are from.

---

10. McKibben, *Deep Economy: The Wealth of Communities and the Durable Future* (New York, NY: Times Books, 2007), 105.

11. Ibid.; also see Brian Halweil, *Eat Here: Reclaiming Homegrown Pleasures in a Global Supermarket* (New York, NY: Norton, 2004), 11–12.

LET US BREAK BREAD TOGETHER

Christians, like the community in Corinth, used to eat meals together regularly, perhaps every night. Those meals would often include the practice of communion, and that practice helped them form a sense of place, a sense of belonging. In the passages I shared in this essay, that place was Corinth, a place that posed its own particular difficulties. The Corinthians were staggering under the revelation that in Christ all are equal (Gal. 3:28). People were divided over whether Peter or Paul was the better preacher. People were divided by class. Men and women were struggling for authority. They were facing the complexity of their place.

Someone thinking with the industrial mind would obscure these complexities by letting each person go his or her own way, fracturing the church until it became a specialized, personalized concept. But someone thinking with the mind of the farmer would realize that there could be no place called Corinth without these complexities. She would also recognize that she will never know who she is or what she ought to do if she tries to escape her place. She would, then, pour herself into that place with fervor, as if her very existence were on the line. She would shape it and it would shape her.

In this regard, trying to think and live according to the mind of the farmer seems to have an awful lot in common with what Paul calls the "mind of Christ" (1 Cor. 2:16). This mind does not fantasize about its place in the stars; it seeks to deeply embed itself in its place. Although Christ may have wandered without a home, he is still God incarnate, the God called Jesus of Nazareth. He is the same God who wept over a place called Jerusalem. He loved that place. Now we, as the body of Christ, must work at living together, "united in the same mind" (1 Cor. 1:10 RSV), to know our place and ourselves. When we break bread together, as the Corinthians did, we are given the opportunity to consider our place and who we are in it, to learn the many complexities and the many gifts inherent to our place. By breaking bread together, we are practicing the reverse movement that Wendell Berry describes; we are "establishing complex local cultures with strong communal memories and traditions of care." If we continue to eat fast food, alone in our cars, we will continue to struggle to know where we are, but if we consistently break bread together, we might just have a shot at being renewed by the transformation of our minds and so discover where and who we are in the process.

Forget escaping to space. Let's break bread instead.

5 Tit for Tat

by T. M. LAWSON

What are you doing here?
Words reserved for my mother
I say now to the mirror.

Looking glass: fairness unchallenged,
except by this earth and fire,
I buried deep, my two burning

stones of wood, observing the dying
embers inherited in my blood. Me,
clothed in my mother's body, sheep

inside wolf, pacing, always
the same story: these curves never left,
like bronze belts, hoisted around hips, thighs,

bellies—I am myself, I am a wicked
stranger, I am a familiar guest with
no host. She can see

through the mirror, even when I look
away, even when I veil
with smoke and powder, these stones

melt. *She knows me*, I menace
to flower petals, plucking—*she knows me not*.
Even as a girl, she was more child than me,

me more mother than daughter, holes in me
which can't be filled, even with seeds, rocks, this
earth—my soul will always be indented, a debt

which I lower myself into, a pit of her
and I: porous. Poor us. I have known
no allegiance except to a mirror,

life as a captive, a standoff
between stone and wood, fighting off
fire, her grip, my fingers on the porcelain sink.

What are you doing here,
she will say when I meet her
for the last time.

6 Being Pretty

by KATHERINE JAMES

THE PHRASE *BONFIRE OF THE Vanities*, while well-known as the title of Tom Wolfe's 1987 novel, originally referred to an actual bonfire that was set on February 7, 1497, in Florence, Italy. The fire was lit by religious fanatics for the purpose of burning objects that a priest had deemed occasions of sin. The objects included art, cosmetics, and books.

I am a condemned soul.

I can imagine one of these fires in my own backyard, flames reaching into the night with my favorite books and art as kindling. Fifteenth-century Christians would have found my idea of the perfect birthday gift—a day at the ubiquitously phallic Museum of Modern Art—to be the very definition of an occasion of sin. But my true vice, the thing that would give the fire muscle and heat, has always been more of the Maybelline sort. I go for eyeliner and lipstick and anything that might make my aging body reflect—however poorly—those women in magazines with full lips and legs better measured by meters than feet.

With Florentine flames as far from my mind as the east is from the west, I recently wandered into a Target and, against my better judgment, decided a few outfits were worth the trouble of trying on. My first mistake was pulling them off the rack two sizes too small. I tend toward these types of miscalculations, possessed by a younger version of myself, as though I'm still that girl who climbed the high dive at the public pool without the least bit of self-consciousness and then mustered enough wherewithal to jump, however awkwardly, into the deep end, swimsuit riding up my butt and all. I swam face down with snorkel and mask, lay on my red-white-and-blue bicentennial towel smeared with enough suntan oil to start a car, and then ran around the deck to the deep end and dove for quarters with friends.

But I'm not that ten-year-old, and the mirrors at Target have been nabbed from a carnival fun house—I'm sure of it. They reflected a spectacularly distorted comedy of myself, and as I shoved one leg into a pair of jeans I thought of the J.Crew catalog I had thumbed through that morning—why do catalogs always refer to pants in the singular? I imagined trying on clothes in one of the attractively lighted J.Crew stores and asking the helpful customer service associate to please get me a size 10 *pant* instead of an 8 *pant*. I'm looking for a khaki *pant*.

Under the florescent lights, I continued to yank my leg into the jeans. On the rack they'd looked like a nice cross between skinny jeans and mom jeans, but no, they weren't, most definitely not. I peeled them off, didn't bother with the two dresses I still hadn't tried on, exited the dressing room, passed my red Target cart with the leatherette belt I took twenty minutes to pick out, and ran out of the store. I might have had a few tears in my eyes, but whatever.

I can't seem to quell the vanity thing. It's always there, staring me down like a photo of Angelina Jolie at a checkout counter. And it's not the size of my clothes so much as the way my white legs have shifted direction, like the way antique glass in an old home ever so slowly slopes and gives in to the waves of time.

I remember as a young girl seeing my grandmother lounging next to a pool in a swimsuit. She loved to swim and appeared comfortable in her time-weathered body, which had folds and sags that I had never seen before. I don't imagine I'll be as confident as her as I continue to age. Even now, I decline my critical vitamin D needs, refusing to visit any sun-kissed place that requires swimwear. Even a Land's End suit doesn't cut it, as hard as they've tried. And don't get me wrong, I do appreciate the wide straps and "thinning" colors. Thank you, Land's End. Really. You tried, and that's the least you could do.

I am a vain, vain woman.

Estrogen has been called the fountain of youth, yet every day I take a cancer pill that depletes my body of estrogen. Forget menopause, my treatment sucks dry every nook and cranny where I imagine cappuccino size dregs of the scared hormone hiding. The fountain of youth has dried up, and I'm scared. But what scares me isn't the cancer returning; it's the appearance of my face. I might become ugly.

In fact, I have found myself—and this is very hard to admit—in front of the bathroom mirror, thumbs at my temples, pulling my skin smooth, imagining what I might look like if the reconstruction surgeon who performed my mastectomy did a little extra something-something while I was under the knife to correct thing number one and thing number two. Right now my breasts have the unfortunate look of an older Pontiac with those closing-flap headlights they used to make, one flap stuck half way up in a sorry wink.

I've always wanted to be one of those super confident women who grow their hair long and gray, who compost and tend their vegetable garden and then go inside and write a few poems before lunch. A confident woman would not be obsessed with her physical features; she could care less about cosmetics. A confident woman would dive for the novels and art before they burned.

But alas, I am a vain, vain woman. Forget the rest, I'd jump in the flames to grab whatever precious vial passed as a cosmetic in 1497. In 1497 I would have been burned at the stake.

The sin of vanity seems to have withstood the test of time, even in my own life. I thought these things were taken care of. In college, at the tender age of nineteen, I changed the course of my life and began focusing on the things that I believed really mattered like, say, eternal life and love and my father in heaven who will one day introduce me to real beauty. Everything looked pretty cool on the surface—all that estrogen and Sun In and those awesome Levi's 501 jeans. However, even then, a great mass of insecurity and self-doubt was submerged within me.

A year ago I found out I had breast cancer. After a mammogram, and then another mammogram, I was led in my pink gown to a small room with no windows and, I swear, no less than twelve tissue boxes. I sat there, beginning to feel like something was definitely up, until a nurse came in and sat down across from me.

"Are you OK?" she asked.

I said, "Apparently not," and thus began my tumble into the world of pink things and breast cancer.

There was a two-week period after my diagnosis in which the forty or so years that I assumed I had left to live (I come from good genetic stock so ninety seemed about right) all of a sudden became three or four. My life—or more precisely, my death—felt five inches from my face, and all I could do was call out to the Lord for more years, plead that he would save me and that my cancer wouldn't kill me. And God said yes. After a double mastectomy and many reconstructive surgeries, as well as medicine that I swear was concocted from bat urine and swamp sludge, my nodes are clear, my tests continue to show zero cancer, and my oncologist tells me my prognosis is excellent.

But trip wires averted, when I look in the mirror now—even with the reconstructive surgeries—my chest is a gnarly mess. It's just plain ugly.

So here I am again. I understand that my worth is found in Christ and not in physical beauty, but believe it or not I can still go there; I can still feel insecure and turn to vain things rather than Christ. I can focus on myself and how I look, or how bad I look with my cancer-marred body, which in turn can make me feel self-critical and insecure, just as I used to feel proud when I felt pretty.

But God's aware of my insecurity, and he's right here, and I'm his child, and what child, especially to her father, is not beautiful?

It's a matter of paying attention, I think. Of not doing the idol thing. When I pay attention to what God communicates in Scripture about how much he loves and cares for me, I'm reminded that he is the one who makes me beautiful. He's continually at work sanctifying and purifying me. Christ in me is a beautiful thing. 1 Peter 5:6–7 says, "Humble yourselves, therefore, under the mighty hand of God so that at the proper time he may exalt you, casting all your anxieties on him because he cares for you" (ESV). This verse could have been written especially for me. When I'm trying on an ill-fitting pair of jeans, anxious about all kinds of worldly nonsense, it reminds me to be humble. I'm already in the habit of casting my anxieties about cancer on God, but this verse reminds me to cast my anxieties about the silly things on God too, to give him all my grief about physical beauty. God cares for me. When I reflect on his love, I don't feel a need to default to the physical beauty that the world values. My pretty, tan body on the high dive so many years ago recedes farther and farther into the past as I look forward to Christ *exalting me at the proper time* and unveiling my true beauty.

Cancer is one way God has graciously (yes, graciously) helped me see myself as beautiful, to see his vision for love, grace, and peace refracted in me. God didn't cause my cancer, but he allowed it, knowing that he would use it for greater purposes.

Without estrogen, I'm not as pretty as I was before the cancer. There's a lot of hair in the drain when I take a shower, and the wrinkles are coming fast and furious. I struggle with this, especially in a time when beautiful women seem to be around every corner with their ten thousand teeth and airbrushed (let's just assume) torsos. It can sometimes feel like those moments in the Gospels when Jesus—almost oddly—says "I tell you the truth" over and over, like he knows beforehand we'll keep forgetting something important he told us years ago and seek beauty from a Target mirror instead of from him.

2 Corinthians 3:18 says, "But we all, with unveiled face beholding as in a *mirror* the glory of the Lord, are transformed into the same image from glory to glory, even as from the Lord, the Spirit." I will one day be beautiful and it will have nothing to do with the tightness or youthfulness of my physical face. It will have everything to do with my reflection of *him,* my *God,* my *Father,* my *Savior.* All praise to the great healer of my soul and my body. I am his bride, and he will have the most beautiful bride.

So I'm glad, in the end, for my estrogen-less body and all that comes with it. There is a way, it turns out, to toss my Maybelline eyeliner in the fire with the books and art and to actually be thankful. It's a wonder to me that much of my beauty in heaven depends on my fading physical beauty. The less attractive I become in the world, the more attractive I become in his eyes, because in cutting off my estrogen he is cutting off my idol. He is pruning me, and even though I might have to wait a bit, it's worth it because I'll be so freaking pretty.

Pilar Timpane, *Lorah in the Field*, Santa Barbara, CA, 2015, digital photograph. Courtesy of the artist.

7 Elena Ferrante's Words Are Good Enough

by TAYLOR ROSS

*Words are good enough. It is idle to fault a net for having holes,
my encyclopedia notes.*

—MAGGIE NELSON, *THE ARGONAUTS*

LAST FALL, AFTER MANY years of purposeful anonymity—this in spite of the recent commercial and critical success of her four-part series, the Neapolitan novels—the Italian author known as Elena Ferrante had her identity exposed in a piece published by the *New York Review of Books*.[1] As Claudio Gatti, the investigative reporter responsible for the unmasking, notes at the beginning of his article, speculation about the true identity of the author behind the pen name has turned a near constant rumor mill since the publication of Ferrante's first book in 1992. It is, indeed, difficult to tell the story of her success, especially over the past two years, without considering the allure of her pseudonymous status. Here was a quartet of books, the breadth and brilliance of which we simply had not yet seen in the new millennium, and we did not even have a real name to praise or a definitive biography to study. There was no body on which we could append our accolades and prestigious medals of artistic acclaim—the makings of a literary mystery.

---

1. Gatti, "Elena Ferrante: An Answer?" *New York Review of Books*, October 2, 2016. https://www.nybooks.com/daily/2016/10/02/elena-ferrante-an-answer/

But it seemed difficult, at times, not to experience this anonymity as lack—not that Ferrante was somehow obligated to reveal herself or that we the readers were having our rights infringed upon by being barred access to the intimate details of her life. What this absence prompted was, rather, something more like the desire to thank the donor of an anonymous gift, or maybe like that feeling Heidegger discovered when he realized we could never catch a full glimpse of Being before it receded ever further behind the beings it gives. Or perhaps it felt something more like how Gregory of Nyssa describes Moses's yearning after only seeing God's backside—the romance of concealment. Like all beautiful gifts, though, there was of course something of the giver imbued in the very words of the Neapolitan novels themselves. "From the greatness and beauty of created things comes a corresponding perception of their creator," says the writer of the Book of Wisdom (13:5 NRSV).

This is true of Ferrante's novels even if the eponymous heroine of her stories is not the exact literary incarnation of the author herself. I know Elena Ferrante, as I know any of my favorite authors, through the texture of her words, the cadence of her sentences, the rhythms of her chapters. I do not need the corroboration of the signified to trust my intimacy with these signifiers. This is to say something about what books are and what they are not. It is to say something about what *these* books are. To think of Ferrante's novels as artifacts that obscure their author is to miss the point. It is to actively avoid what we have been given. A book, like a word, is an expression of its author. It cannot help but be an expression of its author. A book, to put it more strongly still, *expresses* its author, extends her along its pages, carries her beyond her intentions, reveals her to the new worlds its pages create. If you want to know an author, there is nowhere else to look but the words she has written. Wittgenstein would call this a *grammatical* remark.

That this should be so—that this cannot help but be so—is what makes Gatti's painstaking attempt to uncover Ferrante's identity seem so misguided. One wonders at what expense his own reading of the book suffered because of it. There is surely something approaching sacrilegious about reading these four masterpieces of modern prose as ledgers against which to judge financial records. But whatever his reading habits, it appears obvious that Gatti missed Ferrante's many blistering stories of the power of capital, of the seizure of human flourishing by capital, and of the reduction of life itself to capital—like the reduction of a book to pay stubs. (Painfully obvious, too, is Gatti's failure to notice Ferrante's many examples of the manifold ways in which self-deception is something of an occupational hazard for the journalist.)

But that Gatti's procedure is misguided, and perhaps pitiable, makes it no less reprehensible. To think of an author's words as so many masks behind which she hides is not without ethical consequences. Such a perspective registers a kind of skepticism with regard to what words can do and what language can actually accomplish.

It marks a certain disappointment with the body of an author's text. It suggests that the text must be surpassed—gotten behind, gotten under, pulled aside, pulled apart—in an effort to find its true source, the author, as she existed in the fullness of that moment before her thoughts gave birth to the bastard offspring of words. The main problem with this particular picture of language is that, inevitably, it bears violent fruit. And this happens every time a reader mortgages the meaning of an author's words to the intimate details of the life that produced them and so binds the body of the text to the hands that wrote it.

As Aaron Bady put it in his essay on the Gatti article at the *New Inquiry*, for readers who hold this kind of a skeptical stance, the type "who believe themselves to traffic in truth, Ferrante's identity is a 'secret.' But it is not. It is a fiction." I take Bady's use of the word *fiction* here to trade outside the positivist parameters that would have it posed in semantic opposition to the word *fact*. For in a very true sense, one that moves outside the binary opposition between fact and fiction, the identity of Elena Ferrante is real and expressed in her novels. That is, Ferrante's identity, to quote Bady again, is not somehow surreptitious:

> A secret is something withheld, something denied to us; a fiction is created, an imagined artifice spun as such. If you think her identity is a *secret*—if you feel that you have a right to know, and you resent her for withholding what is yours—then you might feel yourself justified in piercing that screen. . . . It will be the only thing you can think about, and what you *can* see will cease to seem important. What you don't know, but only suspect, will become the key to everything else.[2]

Bady here describes well the costs of thinking that the body of the text obstructs some authorial essence. The words—and in Ferrante's case, the exceptionally beautiful words—lose out to the more significant question of the secret they supposedly hide. But Bady also captures the violent ends toward which such skepticism can tend and the justifications that often follow. What we can see, the screen on which the words are offered to our gaze, must be pierced and penetrated if we want to know the truth.

In the particular case of Gatti's article, it is difficult not to notice that this violence has a specifically gendered edge. Like his unwitting inattention to her critiques of capital, in his attempt to unmask the pseudonymous female author Gatti also apparently failed to notice Ferrante's sharp and at times painful meditations on the seizure of women's work, intellectual and otherwise, by men. Instead, he unwittingly writes himself into that story. The following words from Gatti read like the sort of defense often heard from perpetrators of sexual violence: "By announcing that she would lie on occasion, Ferrante has in a way relinquished her right to disappear

---

2. Bady, "Ars longa, vita brevis," *New Inquiry*, October 2, 2016, http://thenewinquiry.com/blogs/zunguzungu/ars-longa-vita-brevis/.

behind her books and let them live and grow while their author remained unknown. Indeed, she and her publisher seemed to have fed public interest in her true identity."[3] The last line, in particular, smacks so clearly of the "she was asking for it" argument against victims of rape that the comparison seems banal, but it is certainly no less apt or appalling.

Bady's comments on the folly of imagining Ferrante's identity as a "secret" hidden from view recall, for me, a passage from J. M. Coetzee's devastating novel *Waiting for the Barbarians*: "How natural a mistake to believe that you can burn or tear or hack your way into the secret body of the other!"[4] Coetzee's line here, like his novel as a whole, is about a specific historical moment in which the colonial myth—that particular bodies, particularly different bodies, were an impediment to recognizing an other as human—took such deep roots that its script is still being read, and written, today. Central to this story is a sense of being shut out by the body of an other, an impression of feeling exiled by the seeming opacity of an other's flesh. When we buy into this narrative, violence waits in the wings. Once this myth takes root, we will assume there is something hidden and withheld from us, something the surface of the body cannot provide. We will be conned into thinking that we must pierce the other's surface in order to confirm our suspicions.

We live in a time when the connection between our habits of reading and our life with others has been largely obscured. Too often, we ignore the ways in which our response to the books we read and our habits of response to others around us can bleed in to one another, cutting across the neat boundaries we erect between mind and will. We forget this at our peril. Or, rather, we forget this at our neighbor's peril. Literature, at its best, can remind us of this connection. But it does so precisely by asking whether we can be satisfied with the body of the text, whether we can be satisfied with this body of words alone, whether we can learn to love our words, like our bodies, without grounding their worth in some hidden depth. In this regard, the books of a pseudonymous author like Elena Ferrante only underline something true of all works of art. If we experience the anonymity of the artist as lack—if we find her words, her canvases, her films not enough on their own—then we have only ourselves to blame.

---

3. Gatti, "Elena Ferrante."
4. Coetzee, *Waiting for the Barbarians* (New York, NY: Penguin, 2010), 49.

8   Ta-Nehisi Coates and the Power of Lament

by ZACH CZAIA

FOR SEVEN YEARS I taught English literature and composition at Cristo Rey, a Jesuit high school in Minneapolis, Minnesota. In my last year there, I taught an AP English class to twelfth graders. Almost all of the students in this class—and in the school as a whole—were either Latino or African American. In the particular class I'm remembering, we had just finished a unit on Shakespeare's *Hamlet*.

In order to get my students to support truly arguable (and not merely obvious) thesis statements, I read aloud from a sheet of one-sentence claims about the play. "Hamlet loves Ophelia," I said, and my students, who were standing in the middle of the classroom, walked to one side of the room if they agreed with the statement or to the other if they didn't. They could also hover in the middle if they didn't feel strongly one way or another. A number of these statements provoked the kind of disagreement I was looking for: when I said, "Spying is the way to truth" the class split, as they did when I said, "Ophelia is a good daughter" and "Hamlet is a Christian." There was one statement, however, that produced no disagreement: "We, like Hamlet, live in an unweeded garden." My students, beautiful and hope-filled as they were, had no doubt that our country was as rife with corruption and injustice as Hamlet's Denmark ever was.

Most of our discussion time in the AP class was spent on explicitly literary texts—novels, poems, plays, and short stories—but there were two times that year when students came to me and asked if we could directly address and respond to events occurring in the world around them. The first came in the aftermath of protests regarding the treatment of African American students at the University of Missouri. The second was to respond to the late Antonin Scalia's inflammatory comments regarding the Abby Fisher case, when the Supreme Court justice asserted that perhaps the University of Texas "ought to have fewer" black students.[1]

For both of these news stories, my students felt a direct connection between the news they were reading and their own futures as citizens of the country. They wanted to understand what they were reading better by discussing it as a group. But there was something else as well. They wanted to speak to each other with honest directness about a particular kind of pain they were feeling. Their conversations on these days took the form of a *lament*, and it is a form I think we as a church and culture need to spend more time understanding and practicing. This lament is also at the heart of Ta-Nehisi Coates's recent book, *Between the World and Me*.

What is a lament? We might think of a funeral scene and of the wailing, moaning, and weeping we observe there. This is lament, but I want to add something else as well: for the Christian, true laments always have social and cosmic significance, rooted as they are in the hope that God listens to our cries. As theologian Bryan Massingale argues in his excellent study *Racial Justice and the Catholic Church*, it is hope that causes Christians to resist injustices, to defy unjust authorities and laws.[2]

Words themselves can often constitute defiance and resistance. Consider a biblical example of this in the words of Job, who, after losing almost everything he has—children, land, crops, and health—cries out: "Naked I came forth from my mother's womb, and naked shall I return there. The Lord gave and the Lord has taken away. Blessed be the name of the Lord" (Job 1:21 NAB). Job is a good man. He does not lose faith in God. But as the story progresses, and the friends who visit fail to console him in his distress and suffering, Job's words grow flintier. They have a bite to them. Here is a man who "rescued the poor who cried out for help," who "was eyes to the blind and feet to the lame," who studied "the rights of the stranger" (29:15 and 16). Yet now, for no apparent reason, this good man is laid low.

The reader knows that Satan has decided to test Job and that God has agreed to allow the testing. But Job doesn't know this. His friends don't either, and they assume the worst: that Job has broken faith with God, that he has done something terrible, and that his losses and sufferings are God's just punishment for Job's wrongdoing.

---

1. Stephanie Mencimer, "Justice Scalia Suggests Blacks Belong at 'Slower' Colleges," *Mother Jones*, December 9, 2015, http://www.motherjones.com/politics/2015/12/justice-scalia-suggests-blacks-belong-slower-colleges-fisher-university-texas.

2. See Massingale, *Racial Justice and the Catholic Church* (New York, NY: Orbis Books, 2010).

But Job refuses to acknowledge something that isn't true. He demands to be heard by God, and the words he chooses flare with honest anger.

These words are *laments*, and they hold great power and consolation for those who suffer: "Oh, that I had one to hear my case," Job cries out, late in the book, "and that my accuser would write out his indictment! Surely I should wear it on my shoulder or put it on me like a diadem; of all my steps I should give him an account; like a prince I should present myself before him" (31:35–37). These are risky, defiant, and hopeful words.

During that Scalia discussion I mentioned, one of my senior students said, "I've had white students say to me, 'Oh, you're lucky, it's going to be much easier for you to win that scholarship because you're Latina.' I get so angry at comments like that!" This student went on to say that she did not want to gain entrance to a university because of her ethnicity but rather because she had earned it through her academic performance. She said that her classmate's comments, as well as the ones by Justice Scalia, showed no understanding of the struggles she had faced as a student or of the particular realities facing her family.

As she spoke, my student was unable to hold back her tears. She was articulating what it's like to live a world in which things are not as they should be. And behind those tears was an anger, a Job-like plea, an impatience for things to change.

I doubt very much that my student would talk about her comments as drawing on the language of Job. Likewise, I doubt that Ta-Nehisi Coates would use the language of prophecy to describe his own writing. Nevertheless, I find that as a Christian I cannot make sense of Coates's words—or those of my students—without prophecy, without the body of Christ.

Saint Paul writes in his letter to the Corinthians, "There are many parts, yet one body. The eye cannot say to the hand, 'I do not need you,' nor again the head to the feet, 'I do not need you.'. . . If one part suffers, all the parts suffer with it; if one part is honored, all the parts share its joy" (1 Cor. 12:21 and 26). Coates, following the insights of James Baldwin, reveals that American racism damages the *whole* of the civic body, not just those who are oppressed. White people—or, better yet, those who "believe they are white," as Coates puts it—are impoverished by the poverty and mistreatment of black people. This insight, which echoes Nelson Mandela, Baldwin, and Martin Luther King Jr., recognizes the central principle of Paul's message and the gospel itself: to overlook the pain and suffering of one of your brothers or sisters is to overlook your own pain and suffering. As the poet and churchman John Donne famously wrote, "Never send to know for whom the bell tolls. It tolls for thee." To refuse to recognize the suffering of one's brothers and sisters is to be deaf to the tolling of the bell.[3]

But lament has the capacity to bring hearing to the deaf. When one is truly a listener in these situations, one enters into the suffering of another person. The listener can be moved to the same anger and desire for change that animate the speaker. Rather than burning bridges between people as we might expect, true lament builds us up through its honest expression of human pain and suffering.

Coates has made it clear in his writing and public speaking that he is not a religious person, and in *Between the World and Me*, he acknowledges that he does not believe in God. And yet his book seems to draw on the biblical sense of lament. It tells the intimate story of how racism has affected his life and the life of his community, and like Job, he refuses to acknowledge that anything in this situation is as it should be. Like Job, Coates cries out for witnesses. He calls to his son and to us, his readers, urging us to find our own connections to his situation, our own places to stand in defiance of injustice.

In one of the closing passages of the book, I was surprised to find Coates openly admiring the faith of a Christian. Reflecting on Mabel Jones's response to the unjust killing of her son—who was also a classmate of Coates—by an undercover police officer, Coates writes of Christianity: "I thought of my own distance from an institution that has, so often, been the only support for our people. I often wonder if in that distance I've missed something, some notions of cosmic hope, some wisdom beyond my mean perception of the world, something beyond the body, that I might have transmitted to you. I wondered this, at that particular moment, because something beyond anything I have ever understood drove Mable Jones to an exceptional life." Coates explains that like his parents before him, he has not transmitted faith in God to his son, the *you* in this passage, but he acknowledges the potential existence of "something beyond anything [he] has ever understood."[4] In his desire to teach his son how to live well in this world, he will not reject anything that is good.

There are critics of *Between the World and Me*—some of them Catholic, for instance Don Wycliff and Rusty Reno—who see Coates as dour or pessimistic. I disagree. Coates is a poet who turns the earth of his imagination with the real. He is an embodied black man who accepts Malcom X's call toward the body and the prevention of its suffering. Again and again, Coates asks us to consider broken black bodies. But he doesn't ask us as his teachers at the public school in Baltimore asked. His ask is a cry. His ask is a lament. Of his slain Howard classmate Prince Jones, Coates writes, "There are people whom we do not fully know, and yet they live in a warm

---

3. Coates, *Between the World and Me* (New York City, NY: Spiegel and Grau, 2015), 42; and Donne, "Meditation XVII," in *Devotions Upon Emergent Occasions and Death's Duel* (Ann Arbor Paperbacks: University of Michigan Press, 1957), 108–9.

4. Coates, *Between the World and Me*, 139.

place within us, and when they are plundered, when they lose their bodies and the dark energy disperses, that place becomes a wound."[5] This wound is not a source of bitterness for Coates, as Catholic reviewers like Reno and Wylcliff argue, but rather a source of insight.

When I was eleven years old, I first read the book *Black Like Me*. This was the story of a white journalist, John Howard Griffin, who had the pigment of his skin artificially darkened. He underwent this experiment so that he could understand more fully what it meant to be a black man in the United States. Whenever I share information about Griffin—as I have sometimes with the students of color whom I've taught—I am quick to point out that, yes, Griffin had the ability to *choose* to "be black" for a time, as a person of color does not have the ability to choose to "be white." He passed as black and then was able to pass back to being white once the ultra-violet treatments and the effects of the skin-darkening drug began to wear off after about six months.

This fall I am not teaching at Cristo Rey. I have spent almost ten years with teenagers—primarily teenagers of color—and I've now decided to take a break. I feel burned out, as if I've used up my capacity for this particular kind of work. The experience has changed me, and I wouldn't trade it for the world, but like Griffin, I am ready to step away. And like Griffin, I recognize that this ability to step in and out—to move, to change—is a luxury. My brothers and sisters of color cannot shrug off the difficulties associated with their skin; few of them can simply leave a neighborhood that is killing them or their loved ones.

But no teacher ever leaves teaching completely behind. And I don't think that any of us can afford *not* to teach, especially in this moment in our history. The more I read him, the more certain I am that what Coates is doing throughout his writing is what I have been trying to do in my daily work. He is teaching. He is teaching his son about the world and the way he has survived here, but he is also teaching his readers. He has taught me that language's power is not measured strictly by its ability to create a policy or movement. Rather, it is a capacity in the heart and the mind to understand a person different from yourself. In an interview with the journalist Ezra Klein after Coates published his *Atlantic* piece, "The Case for Reparations," Coates asked Klein, "What happened to imagination? Not the world we live in but the world we want to live in?"

I hear those lines, and I think of my students. These students may or may not have heard of Coates, but they don't need Coates to know that, for them, there has always been something a little unreal about the American dream. Last fall, they turned on a television and considered the candidates for president of the United States, and in

---

5. Ibid., 64.

one party, the leading candidate proposed deporting all undocumented immigrants *en masse*. They went to their workplaces and heard their supervisors supporting this candidate. Astonishingly, this candidate has now become the president. They are in college now, those AP English students. I know they read the news. It seems like every month there is a new case of a young unarmed black man who has been killed by police forces. I know my students read these stories. Sometimes the stories are complex and require investigation to understand exactly what has occurred; sometimes they are exactly what they appear to be: the brutal exercise and enforcement of power over the powerless. My students have the need to lament these situations as Coates has. If any of them are to be prophetic in the way our Judeo-Christian tradition has thought of prophecy, we need to give them the space and training to speak their laments, and if need be, to groan or shout them until they are heard.

9 Sing More Like a Girl

by Sus Long

I'VE SPENT A LOT of time watching men's mouths. Matching vowel shapes. Anticipating the intake of breath and the clip of the final consonant. To be a backup singer is to make the principle sound good. I do not distract. I do not show off. I harmonize. If I'm doing my job, you're looking at me, but you're listening to him. You know, *him*. The man with the microphone.

I recently started teaching two of the guys in my band to sing harmony. I still can't believe that sentence—that I have a band, that we book clubs and go on tour, that three incredibly talented, good-looking men stand behind me while we play songs that I wrote. They listen to my ideas and write instrumental parts; they practice on their own time, and then, in front of breathing, beer-drinking concert-goers, they let me stand up front at the microphone and sing the lead.

I even have a woman who sings backup for me. She watches my mouth and breathes when I breathe and she makes the principle sound good. I don't have to explain anything to her about her function as one-who-harmonizes, but I'm finding that with the guys I have to explain everything. They get frustrated that they don't intuitively know how to sing harmony—and, sure, it's a skill that takes years of practice—but it's also something that seems to go along with being raised a girl. It occurs to me that a little girl will sing more harmony because harmony is what's expected in every aspect of her life. She's watching his mouth. She's adjusting to make him sound better. Even if you can't nail the tune, I tell the boys, it's most important to start when I start, stop when I stop, and match my vowel shapes. They don't understand, so I say it again, "You have to sing without listening primarily to yourself—you should be listening to *me*."

For most of my life my father worked in the music industry as a producer, so I spent a good chunk of my childhood haunting concerts I didn't care about. That's the rule, right? No matter how cool your dad's job is, it's a developmental imperative that you think it's stupid. He took me and my sister to hear Diana Krall in the park and Point of Grace in the amphitheater, and these women spun on the stage like ballerinas in a jewelry box—poised, pressed, shiny. I was sharply aware of the glamour and nonsense of women who looked so smooth onstage and so jagged afterwards, up close, with their raccoon eyes and nicotine teeth. I recall being small and making a rude comment about the haircuts of the Manhattan Transfer while visiting their dressing room. Even as a very young know-it-all, I knew this was not my scene.

Then at thirteen, I found myself at the Warfield in San Francisco for my first rock concert. I didn't know the band or anything about their music. I was merely tagging along with my friends, following someone else's musical taste into a club, just as I had with my dad. We were four, barely-teenage girls, crammed between groping couples and old people sneaking hits off a palmed joint, and when it got hot on the dancefloor, I had to tie my windbreaker around my waist—yes, my windbreaker, because it was 2003 and I was a kid from the burbs. The music was loud. The lead singer of the opening band spit beer on us, and when my slippery jacket was finally jostled to the floor, it was swept away and tossed into the air, back and forth like a beach ball. Between bands I tilted my face to the ceiling and tried to get fresh air. Everything was covered in sweat. I wasn't sure what all the fuss was about.

But then the fuss found me. The Hives came on in their crisp suits and bolo ties, Howlin' Pelle Almqvist working the gaunt, contortionist look, literally swinging from the ceiling at one point, overwhelmed with his own internal fire. I had never seen anything like it. I thought my heart was going to explode. It was like the most head-spinning first kiss, like losing track of the surface of the ocean beneath the crush of a wave. Someone had let these men get up on a stage and amplify something profound and personal and internal. They played wildly; they shouted; they soaked through their clothes. Pelle called us "goddamn fucking hippies," and we screamed for more.

Once I'd gotten my feet and stopped spinning and smiling and feeling wonderfully high, I started to cry. I could not possibly have articulated it then, but I knew, at thirteen, standing in my Chuck Taylors, my windbreaker flying across the room, that this was not something I'd ever get to do. The swaggering and the sweating and the bellowing, playing your guitar until your fingers bled, mouthing off into a microphone—it broke my baby heart to find out that there was something so sublime in the world and that I'd never know what it felt like. I went home and was depressed for days. How do you become a rock star? How do you ask other people to play your music, and then how do you ask other people to listen?

It wasn't at home that I got the idea that I couldn't be Pelle. Our walls were decorated with pictures of Sarah Vaughn and Ella Fitzgerald and Rosemary Clooney. My parents insisted that I play an instrument from the time I was four, and they encouraged me as I butchered the piano and trumpet and guitar and electric bass. My mother comes from a large Mennonite family, and they like to kick off their meals with the doxology sung in four-part harmony—women sing in this family. Women sang in that house. We watched a lot of *The Lawrence Welk Show*, and everyone knew Norma Zimmer was in charge.

But still. Surrounded by a host of strong, singing, female role models, there was a lightness to them that I didn't see in myself—not just in the mirror—but that I didn't resemble deep in my chest. Those pretty words they crooned were not the harsh, ugly things that tumbled out in my own poetic efforts. I wrote deviant things. I kept secrets. I worried that I harbored the insurgence of those spindly, craggy rock n' rollers within the soft arms and round belly of my grandmother. The two parts could not be reconciled.

I spent my high school years as one of those loose, dramatic choir kids. I embraced my station as an alto, high priestesses of harmony, and met the girl who would be the other half of my first band, a comedy duo called Pretty Girls in High Heels. We were awkward and inappropriate and very bad at guitar, but we'd write joke songs about our friends and perform them in public. Poorly. And to the great offense of almost everyone who was referenced therein. There was something significant, of course, in the name we chose for our not-so-serious band. We grew up in the age of Britney and Christina and Beyoncé. We knew that we weren't sexy or edgy—we were not pretty girls in high heels—and so our musical aspirations, like our music, were just a joke.

This friend of mine was also the child of a musician, and she knew what I knew—women are allowed in front as long as they are indisputably talented and pleasingly decorative. While our male classmates formed bands and played shitty venues and were allowed to try and fail, we made our already-failure into comedy. We knew exactly what we were not—we were not yet perfect. This is the rite of passage: When boys form a band, they make a lot of noise before the noise gets very good. It takes a lot of practice to learn to turn yourself inside out. But when a girl makes her first appearances onstage, it is always about how she looks. Hair and makeup, posture and grace. She doesn't make a lot of noise, and no one assumes she has a point of view to express or that she's struggling to learn to express herself at all. In fact, we ask her to please keep the inside inside, to make entertainment out of what is on the outside.

The director of the high school musical told me: "You had the better callback, but you don't look right for the lead."

For as long as I submitted myself to the approval of casting directors, to cliquey college a cappella auditions, to the tyranny of music magazines, and to the authority of every Jack Johnson wannabe around the campfire, I continued to look wrong for the lead. And it broke me. In college, I hung up my identity as a performer and set out to look for mentors in literature. I once crashed a private reading at my university by Beth Lisick, whose most recent book I had read and reread like a roadmap for being a woman who just doesn't give a shit. Afterward, I went up to her, clutching my copy of her memoir, and asked with saucer-eyed intensity, "Who gave you permission?"

Of course, she thought I was insane and asked kindly, "Permission to do what?" I stretched out my arms, at a loss. "Just permission. Who told you that you were allowed to do this? For your life?" I think she said something gracious about having supportive parents, but the wheels were already turning in my head. I was struck by the way she'd repeated the word *permission* as if she'd never been stalked and brutalized by the idea. It wasn't just about looking wrong and not being able to have a music career because I didn't see anyone who resembled me at the front of a stage. I had been blaming my body, but there was a deeper impediment. There was, in my mind, an unbreakable association between being pleasing to look at and being worth listening to. And no matter what I didn't eat, no matter the laps around the east field track, I would never cross the magical threshold where I would be beautiful enough to receive permission. I had misunderstood the power of that casting director—the only person withholding permission was me.

I don't think it's a coincidence that I started to make peace with my body around the same time that I started writing serious songs and letting people hear them. I wish I could say it was some sort of holistic, enlightened revelation in which I embraced my physical self and was rewarded with a vast and fertile creative landscape. I wish I could say that I walked out of that book reading that day and wrote myself a giant permission slip and tacked it over my bed.

It was almost the opposite. I finally saw the hole into which I had slipped and the steep walls I'd have to climb. I deteriorated. I stopped sleeping. I refused to take care of myself—to eat, to change my clothes. I would stay up all night and then throw myself into the Pacific Ocean at dawn, freezing my body until I couldn't move my fingers. Nineteen and I already felt ninety, brittle and exhausted, sucked under by a depression that I couldn't shake or name.

At my most terrified, I huddled on the floor of my apartment and—as if this were the most natural response to fierce mental illness—I wrote a song. And it was a

Jennifer Jane Simonton, *Susannah Long*, Fidelitorium Recording Studio, NC, 2017, digital photograph. Courtesy of the artist.

true song that said true things. It felt like I'd drilled a small hole in my troubled mind and that the ghosts were finally escaping. It was only then, when I first grabbed hold of that lifeline, when I understood the connection between this work and survival, that "looking right" became immaterial. It would be enough work just to learn to stay alive.

That was seven years ago. That first tiny hole became a fissure that runs the length of my body. I can trace my fingers along it. I can peel back the skin. I have spent every day since learning to turn myself inside out without hurting anyone. Without hurting me. And the desire of my bandmates to learn harmony has become an act of compassion, as much as an act of performance.

We played our first real gig as a band in April 2015. It was a forty-five-minute slot at a popular local venue, and we knew there would be a lot of people there, some were even coming to see us. One of my bandmates, the female vocalist, asked, "What do you want me to wear?" I'd been thinking about it for weeks. I told our guitarist that I didn't want to do that female-front thing where I'm in a dress and heels and the guys are all casual. "If it ain't broke, don't fix it," he said, only sort-of kidding. We arrived at the venue, the day of the show, without having made a decision about how we all ought to look. I wore jeans and a T-shirt for sound check. We rushed through load-in in the pouring rain, and I felt superhuman to be lugging amps up flights of stairs, smeared with water and sweat, finally rolling up my sleeves and working for this thing in a new way.

When we were all inside, the doorman walked up to the guitarist and handed him a wristband. "These are for you guys," he said, handing one to our bass player and one to the drummer, "and then I can give the wives hand stamps in a minute." He nodded at me and turned to walk away. Of course, it made absolutely no difference what I wore. Or how ardently I demonstrated that I could do the heavy lifting. I could have chosen the biggest prom dress, the tightest black leather pants. I could have added a baseball cap to my twelve-year-old-boy ensemble, and that man would still have assumed it wasn't my band. Three dozen gigs later, I still can't convince most sound engineers to do what I ask, and the club owners tend to shake hands with my male bandmates first.

But that's me looking at the problem from the wrong angle again. What I wear to a gig doesn't matter. I'll never win the legitimacy that my male counterparts are handed without question, but that's not why my wardrobe doesn't matter. It doesn't matter because the work of being a performer is to stand at the front of a room and transform—to offer the whole self, turned inside out, a body alive with violations, something grotesque made beautiful.

©Lia Chavez

10 Performativity and the Flesh: The Economy of the Icon in Lia Chavez's *Light Body*

by JULIE M. HAMILTON

MIDWAY THROUGH PAOLO SORRENTINO's visually sumptuous and Felliniesque film *The Great Beauty*, a grand soiree is held at a Roman estate.[1] There, a young artist is forced by her parents to perform and paint before a live audience. The guests are among Italy's most esteemed patrons. Through her tears, she paints for greedy eyes, becoming a marketable commodity exploited by her wealthy parents. The decadent fete is a painful tableau, inviting the gaze of the guests to ogle the uncomfortable spectacle. Critiquing the bacchanal, the protagonist Jep Gambardella perceives the frantic desperation beneath the glittering surfaces of high society—the "blah, blah, blah," as he calls it—and exits the noisy affair. In this scene, Sorrentino shows us performance art's perpetual threat of devolving into spectacle—a beauty that is deeply damaged and objectified—while concurrently illustrating its powerful potential to serve as icon.

This essay considers the recent performance *Light Body* by the artist Lia Chavez, a practitioner of contemporary performance and embodied art.[2] Chavez employs ascetic disciplines, meditation techniques, and habituated neurological training in hyperconsciousness alongside religious practices culled from Tibetan Buddhism and

---

1. *La Grande Bellezza* ("*The Great Beauty*"), directed by Paolo Sorrentino (Rome, Italy: Indigo Film, 2013), DVD.

2. This essay was adapted from a paper presented at the Association of Scholars of Christianity in the History of Art Symposium, the Union League Club, New York, NY, in February 2017.

Christian mysticism. Her ascetic commitments, I suggest, place her in the historical lineage of monastics and saints, whose lives might be read as early forms of performance art.

Actress and activist Isabella Rossellini commissioned Lia Chavez's *Light Body* as the first performance on her farm in Brookhaven, New York.[3] On an unusually warm July evening, she opened her grounds to host the performance, offering us garden fare and glasses of rosé. The guests were adorned in summer finery—maxi-length florals and crisp, white linens. Each attendee was presented with a handsome catalog that featured Chavez's *Ascent* ink-transfer prints alongside art critic Andrea Codrington Lippke's thoughtful essay *Foolish Fire, Holy Fools and Thoughtful Paths*. At sunset, Rossellini gathered the guests at a semicircle of blankets in a clearing near the edge of the woods. Directing us to sit facing a dirt path, Rossellini invited us to participate in a guided meditation to clear our minds— a practice that she had learned from filmmaker David Lynch, her former partner. As twilight faded into dusk, Rossellini asked us to open our eyes, which needed to adjust to the darkening horizon. Far off in the distance, I spotted several faint flickers of light, like multicolored fireflies.

As I squinted to better observe the beginning of the performance, I found myself frustrated: I could not see the choreographed dance steps, the exquisite costumes, the vibrant makeup. Enshrouded by the forest, the carefully curated performance was hardly perceptible to my naked eyes. Why go to such lengths to create something intricate that simply could not be seen? Slowly, I began to discern three fluid bands of variegated colors swirling in tandem beyond the trees. Barefoot, I got up from my place on the blanket and walked to the edge of the path, trying to see more of this *Light Body*. Gradually, the soft light moved closer toward me, the sounds of cicadas and crickets wafting through the humid summer air. Three silhouetted figures progressed from right to left, toe-heel, toe-heel, on the unlit path. These three graces moved together in synchronistic unity, as if a single organism, exhibiting the poise of ballerinas. In their lithe arms, LED track lights became effervescent light sculptures, morphing into geometric shapes and genetic helixes.

As I strained to catch sight of the exquisite couture designed by Mary Katrantzou, I began to understand that the limited visibility of the performance was not an oversight. In initially struggling to grasp the vision of light and make sense of what I was seeing, I found myself witnessing a phenomenon yet nonetheless unable to apprehend the thing seen. As my eyes adjusted, however, I began to see each dancer separately: Lia Chavez, Troy Ogilvie, and Djassi daCosta Johnson, each appareled differently. Their heavy breathing increased as they moved toward me—spinning,

---

3. Chavez, *Light Body*, July 23, 2016, live dance performance by Lia Chavez, Djassi deCosta Johnson, and Troy Ogilvie at Brookhaven Hamlet, NY, commissioned by Isabella Rossellini, presented by Beverly Allan and Nur Elektra El Shami, featuring costumes by Mary Katrantzou, curated by Tali Wertheimer, and photographed and documented by Ira Lippke.

reeling, twirling, sculpting the night air with kaleidoscopic lassoes, their bands imprinting afterimages of light in the night sky. Finally, the trio of sweaty dancers paused and faced us in a staggered line. Synchronizing their rainbow bands in 360-degree spirals, their motions resembled a thurifer, as if they were swinging incense in around-the-world clockwork circles. A sumptuous mise-en-scène.

Lia Chavez is always performing. Whether she is meditating in a gallery for eight hours on end, not speaking for forty days, collaborating with neuroscientists in a London laboratory, or meeting me for cocktails at the Mercer Hotel, she knowingly conducts her dancer-like form on the stage of the world and is perfectly herself. Indeed, she seems to inhabit a mythic and fantastical realm—adorned in caftans and headdresses, dramatic eye makeup swathed on her alabaster complexion. Far from pretentious, her effervescence and warmth are disarming, her sincerity and hospitality lush. I am continually surprised by the unforeseen excess of her radiant presence, exuding a beauty that nurtures me.

Even her home adds to this sense of theatrical cohesiveness. The newly renovated house and studio on Long Island functions like a James Turrell light sculpture. A floor-to-ceiling vision in soft white, the minimalist architecture features glass skylights between the first and second floors that flood her domestic monastery with Zen-style lighting. The structure acts as a kind of sundial, featuring light more or less prominently at particular stages of the day. That Chavez should transform her dwelling into an installation comes as no surprise: light is her primary medium, other than her own body. Her father studied under Carl Sagan, inculcating her with a love for the celestial heavens and the intersections of science and art. As a result, her knowledge of astronomy and fascination with the cosmos are grounded in serious aesthetic questions about the human body.[4]

Preparation for this commission led Chavez to India to study contemplative walking, the foundation for all other iterations of yoga practice, from the Himalayan yoga and raja-yoga traditions as taught by Swami Rama and Swami Veda Bharati. By reducing yoga to body and breath, this practice unites mindful contemplation and diaphragmatic breathing. Chavez's method incorporates slow walking, toe-to-heel, in equal pace, while simultaneously inhaling one count, exhaling two counts. Mantras, or sacred utterances, are paired with each breath to maintain focus and concentration. Often just a word or sound, these mantras are said in repetition, calming the

---

4. For more on Lia Chavez's use of bodily know-how, particularly in relation to Maurice Merleau-Ponty's notion of *praktognosia* as the body's primary somatic epistemology in ascetic practices and performance art, see my article "Doing as Knowing: The Performance Art of Marina Abramović and Lia Chavez," SEEN 15, no. 2 (2015): 28–33.

mind and opening the heart. Together, these religious prayer patterns form the underlying structure of Chavez's *Light Body* performance.

Returning from her training in India, Chavez took a vow of silence for forty days. These ascetic parameters proved difficult when planning and rehearsing without the aid of verbal communication between Chavez and her production team. Nonetheless, it invited them to engage in creative methods using their bodies as primary vehicles for translation and interpretation. Drawing upon the yogic template, Chavez developed her six-part chorographical method specifically for *Light Body*. First, steps one and two establish the breath and the walk, followed by step three which meters and synchronizes inhalation and exhalation; step four incorporates the mantra "love" with the breath inhalation and the mantras "light" and "surrender" with the exhalation. These mantra-laden breath cycles continue until the dancer is able to advance to step five, what Chavez describes as philosophical contemplation, in which the mind asks the self a question or query and is able to encounter mental and physical release. Ultimately, metaphysical contemplation is possible in step six if the mind and body simultaneously unite as a "moving mantra," wherein, Chavez says, "exertion becomes cathartic and medicinal." Each of these steps gradually builds on the other and is exponentially self-emptying. The overall goal is transfiguration, or enlightenment—the stage associated with "light bodies."[5]

A light body in Tibetan Buddhism describes the electromagnetic fields or "auras" emitted from the body (otherwise described by scientists as neural networks).[6] This rainbow body is a phenomenon ascribed to Buddhist saints and sages in which the body of a holy figure posthumously transforms into rainbows of color, testifying to the saint's transcendence. In Christianity, we might think of the rosary's luminous mysteries, where we encounter the narrative depictions of both the transfiguration and resurrection of Christ. For Chavez, this phenomenological concept of a rainbow body is concretely captured in the prism, a mirror that receives white light and refracts colored light. She has explored iterations of the prism through many mediums prior to *Light Body*, ranging from photographs in *A Thousand Rainbows* to her meditative nightclub installation *The Octave of Visible Light*, all attempting to represent her light visions through artistic forms.

Over a period of years, Chavez has worked extensively with a team of neuroscientists at Goldsmiths, University of London, as the subject for its research associated with creativity in the brain. By allowing neuroscientists to monitor her neural activity under varying states of meditation, Chavez has not only aided in pinpointing the cranial geography of imagination and artistic creativity but also in underlining

---

5. *Light Body* choreographic method as told to me in personal correspondence with Chavez, February 8, 2017.

6. Kelly Crow, "Artist Lia Chavez Lends Her Mind to Science," *Wall Street Journal*, October 18, 2016, https://www.wsj.com/articles/artist-lia-chavez-lends-her-mind-to-science-1476799598.

the distinctive types of waves the brain transmits during meditation.[7] By assessing Chavez's brain-wave correspondence to her spontaneous mental imageries, a team of researchers has been able to map how imagination is linked to creativity in the brain. Practicing two main types of meditation—stabilizing and analytic (as described above)—Chavez achieves gamma-wave states that generate visions akin to "psychedelic phosphine hallucinations."[8] Chavez relates that she witnesses something analogous to the moment of conception—the neurological nexus of artistic creativity. These fractal patterns and "mental meteorologies" as Chavez describes them, echo other forms of conception in the universe: the birth and death of stars, biomorphic phenomena, the growth of organisms, and geometric patterns. From her meditative visions, the research team at Goldsmiths has been able to explore the potential of gamma waves, which scientists are now calling the "dark matter of consciousness."[9] So, we might ask, how do these meditative visions precisely situate Lia Chavez within the contemporary world of performance art? Not only is it through her ascetic practices that she is able to encounter her mental pictures, but her ascetic commitments place her in the historical lineage of monastics and saints, who I suggest might be read as early forms of performance art.

In her book *Postmodern Heretics: The Catholic Imagination in Contemporary Art*, art critic Eleanor Heartney discusses performance artists who borrow from specific religious practices, liturgies, prayers, and bodily disciplines in their work. These artists have been overwhelmingly female—think of Carolee Schneemann, Yoko Ono, and Coco Fusco. Each of these women invokes her body as an ephemeral mode of communication, a text and locus of meaning-making, reacting against patriarchal models of museum collecting, which are primarily object-based.[10] Yet the practices themselves participate in a historical lineage of ascetic disciplines, situated primarily among monastics and saints. By acknowledging performance art's codified evolution out of painting into actions, we might find it fitting to consider an older form of performance that predates the twentieth century, by examining the lives of mystics and holy fools.

Like performance artists, mystics and monastics from the Christian tradition often found themselves in tension with bureaucratic and ecclesial hierarchies, as they employed ascetic and often bizarre practices in efforts to reform the church. With many women occupying these roles (e.g., Hildegard of Bingen, Julian of Norwich,

---

7. Ibid.

8. Andrea Codrington Lippke, *Foolish Fire, Holy Fools and Thoughtful Paths* (New York, NY: Lia Chavez Studio, 2016).

9. Crow, "Artist Lia Chavez."

10. See Heartney, *Postmodern Heretics: The Catholic Imagination in Contemporary Art* (New York, NY: Midmarch Arts, 2004); and Jonathan David Fineburg, *Art since 1940: Strategies of Being* (New York, NY: H. N. Abrams, 1995).

Teresa of Avila), religious women have played significant roles in challenging authoritative influences among their communities. Mystics, monastics, and martyrs read the dramatic narrative of Christ's life as a play to be reenacted and performed, *imitatio Christi*, often quite literally through flagellation, self-mutilation, and excessive fasting. We now see echoes of these actions in works by performance artists such as Marina Abramović, Hermann Nitsch, and Chris Burden (among others). I draw attention to these artists not to claim any sort of value judgment on their actions but rather to acknowledge that *both* saints and performance artists have participated in strange, ritualistic, and often masochistic actions that test the body's endurance and limitations.

In considering this synthetic connection between contemporary performance art, especially in the context of Chavez and her *Light Body*, and the performativity of saint's lives, I am drawn to Gregory of Nyssa's *Life of Macrina*, in which he provides a hagiographic account of his sister Macrina, a fourth-century monastic.[11] Nyssen, a rhetorically trained bishop, reimagines and articulates the virtuous life of his sister as playing the role of Socrates in Plato's *Symposium*, who is the embodied voice of wisdom. Nyssen emphasizes that Macrina's beauty was unsurpassed—she could have married well and had an economically and socially secure life, yet she turns away suitors, devoting her life to her community, her family, the poor, and above all, to God.

At one point in the account, Macrina discovers a dangerous tumor near her heart, but rather than undergo a life-threatening surgical procedure, she *performs* the scene from the Gospels in which Christ heals the blind man. Mixing "a mud salve of earth and tears," she applies it to her breast, and then asks her mother to make the sign of the cross over her breast.[12] She is miraculously healed and the tumor is replaced with a small scar—a sign or stigma of her flesh witnessing to "wounded love." In depicting these events, Nyssen extols Macrina's faith, arguing that her virtues indicate sainthood.

Nyssen also writes of a dream he has before Macrina's passing: "I seemed to be carrying the relics of martyrs in my hand and a light seemed to come from them, as happens when the sun is reflected on a bright mirror so that the eye is dazzled by the brilliance of the beam." With this vision he anticipates her passing, made acutely aware of her life as holy. At sunset before her death, Macrina ends her life with a meditation, offering hymns to God as she witnesses the "beauty of the Bridegroom." As Nyssen observes Macrina's body being prepared for her funeral, he places his

---

11. See Gregory of Nyssa, "The Life of Saint Macrina," in *Saint Gregory of Nyssa: Ascetical Works*, trans. Virginia Woods Callahan, Fathers of the Church, vol. 58 (Washington, DC: Catholic University of America Press, 1967), 163–91.

12. Quoted in Natalie Carnes, *Beauty: A Theological Engagement with Gregory of Nyssa* (Eugene, OR: Cascade, 2014), 242.

mother's veil over her corpse with the help of his sister Vetiana, and observes a unique phenomenon: "In the dark, the body glowed, the divine power adding such grace to her body that as in the vision of my dream, rays seemed to be shining forth from her loveliness."[13] This description of Macrina's corpse is not unlike our discussion of a light body—in that like the virtuous Buddhist figures, her body posthumously glows. Here, Nyssen portrays the body as a medium for divine beauty, a "mirror" reflecting and radiating light.[14]

Natalie Carnes has noted in her book *Beauty: A Theological Engagement with Gregory of Nyssa* that "[Nyssen's] text never lets the reader leave the beauty of bodies. It continually returns to them, the final instance of a beautiful body the most compelling, pointing not to possibilities for worldly acclaim, but to divine power and grace. Macrina's body remains bodily but has been transfigured into a sign of divine presence."[15] Macrina's luminosity cannot be concealed but continues to reveal itself to the witnessing community. Carnes reminds us, however, that Macrina's beauty *is* represented in Nyssen's rhetoric. His textual narration celebrates her body as a kind of text, as a relic and an icon.

Since late antiquity, the icon has served as the primary medium of a visual culture in which religion, art, and politics overlap. Whether they depict Christ, such as *Christ Pantocrator* at St. Catherine's Monastery at Sinai, or Byzantine emperors, like the Justinian and Theodora mosaics at the Basilica of San Vitale in Ravenna, icons make figures present to the viewer. Debates in the eighth century over the legitimacy of representing God in matter raged between the iconoclasts and iconodules. Following theological defenses of the icon by both John Damascene and his protégé Theodore the Studite, the church affirmed that icons are analogous to the incarnation and hypostatic union of Christ's divine and human natures. Thus, the icon's modality is a correspondence between the viewer and the viewed, allowing the gaze of the beholder to ascend to the prototype by means of material and relational representation. In essence, an icon makes present, and indeed, *performs*, what is unseen.

Christian theologians have described the icon as elastic, such that it may be extended to other artistic forms, including the work of poets like Gerard Manley Hopkins and Denise Levertov, composers such as J. S. Bach and James MacMillan, and directors like Andrei Tarkovsky and Ingmar Bergman. But what about performance art? Theater, certainly, is engaged with aspects of incarnation, especially through mimesis, when an actress inhabits a character and performs that character to the degree that she no longer resembles herself. But *performativity* and *embodied art* get

---

13. Ibid, 232 and 186.

14. J. Warren Smith, *Passion and Paradise Human and Divine Emotion in the Thought of Gregory of Nyssa* (New York, NY: Crossroad, 2004), 48. Nyssen uses the language of the *mirror* in his symbolic terminology for the body and the soul.

15. Carnes, *Beauty*, 66.

at something different entirely—the person performing is not concerned with verisimilitude but rather, and perhaps more importantly, with depicting dimensions of the self in a nonfictional, often unscripted manner, in the form of her own human flesh.

Paul Griffiths, who draws from the work of phenomenologist Jean-Luc Marion, provides a helpful schema for understanding the correspondence between icons and flesh in his book *Intellectual Appetite: A Theological Grammar*. An icon, Griffiths writes, represents the beauty of the created order and signifies something other than itself, pointing its viewers to something beyond itself. We might find such iconicity in the inexhaustibility of a human face. In this context, the face functions as a kind of mirror, both to the viewer's gaze and to that which it reflects. When the viewer gazes at this face as icon, what she sees is neither static nor arrested, but nourished—she is thereby seduced deeper into its beauty. For Griffiths, things are iconic in so far as they are close to Christ's body. Sometimes this proximity is intimate, and other times it is distant.[16]

Why should Christ's body have a special relationship to the icon? For the Christian, the fleshly body bears the image of God, and through that incarnation, God has made human flesh iconic, regardless of the damage it has incurred. This conviction that human flesh can never cease to be iconic follows from Augustine's Platonic logic: in so far as something exists, it participates in being and thereby participates in God. To not participate in God is to cease to exist, and one cannot irradiate one's iconicity without remainder. That is to say, one cannot be damaged beyond one's ability to be iconic.[17]

For Griffiths, as for Marion, the flesh is a lived icon that is saturated and inexhaustible: that is to say, the body is a site of overwhelming givenness, a vehicle in time and space of the unforeseen. The face serves as the endless hermeneutic, the visible in excess. The face is not an abstraction or a concept; it is not beauty or idea. The face is envisaged in me. I know a face because I face it.[18] Consequently, the face, and therefore the flesh, is an icon par excellence.

While Chavez does not necessarily share Macrina's forms of *askesis* (i.e., her vow of poverty and virginity), their performative lives are shaped by shared religious practices. As a bearer of human flesh, the saint Macrina participates maximally in the archetype of the icon. Imagining Macrina's life as a performance, we can reconsider Nyssen's narrative in terms of her bodily practices and rituals. She performs her ascetic commitments to poverty, chastity and obedience as a monastic way of life. These disciplines afford her a spiritual intimacy and supernatural wisdom that her

---

16. Griffiths, *Intellectual Appetite: A Theological Grammar* (Washington, DC: Catholic University of America Press, 2009), 192 and 190.

17. Ibid, 191.

18. See Marion, *The Crossing of the Visible*, trans. James K. A. Smith (Stanford, CA: Stanford University Press, 2004).

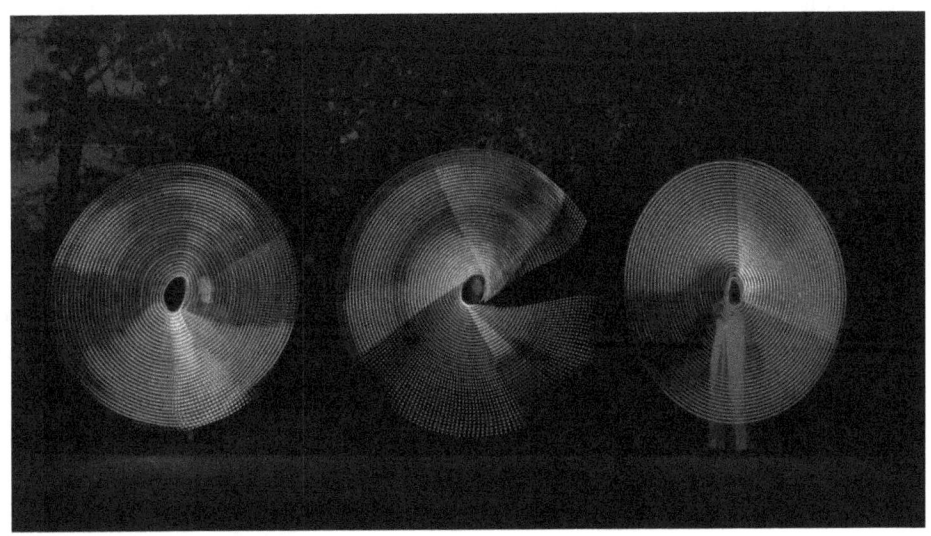

©Lia Chavez

brother notes as praiseworthy and desirable—in fact, Nyssen describes Macrina as his spiritual mother.[19] Her life is iconic because, through her body, it bears witness to something beyond itself. Her body is consecrated as a vessel that exhibits holiness and luminosity.

Chavez too participates in the modality of the icon, intuiting and perceiving mystical experiences, performing them through artistic mediums in the gallery, the forest, and the monastery. By probing the inner landscapes of her mind, she harnesses creative insights that inspire fresh connections between art and science, stemming from religious consciousness. Deploying this consciousness as an artistic material, she offers her flesh as a conduit or mirror, a prism refracting light.

In the final canto of Dante Alighieri's *Paradiso*, the poet describes the experience of beholding a luminous substance, which appears to be three overlapping circles of differing colors in a singular dimension:

> In the deep and bright essence of that exalted Light, three circles appeared to me; they had three different colors, but all of them were of the same dimension; one circle seemed reflected by the second, as rainbow is by rainbow, and the third seemed fire breathed equally by those two circles.[20]

The longer Dante looks into the light, the more his eyes begin to adjust, seeing more clearly. As his gaze intensifies, the light takes on nuance, difference, multivalence, and *color*. Chavez explained to me that "Dante's *Paradiso* has perhaps been the greatest influence to my thinking around light mysticism. . . . It has afforded me a classical and poetic foundation for addressing the paradox occurring when the vision of the natural eyes is fused with the vision of the inner eyes."[21] Through her *Light Body*, Chavez offers us the mystery of light—unharnessable, uncommodifiable, uniquely experienced light, a prism refracting a rainbow. Indeed, Ira Lippke's film documentation of the *Light Body* performance captures the three dancers as a trio of intersecting circles, a multicolored Venn diagram, precisely as Dante has described.

In a letter Gregory of Nyssa writes to Macrina's brother Peter, he discusses the natural phenomenon of the rainbow as an analogy to the Christian claim that God is triune. The prism, he writes, encounters white light, one indivisible substance, and refracts from it a spectrum of colored light: "there occurs a kind of bending and return of the light upon itself, for the radiance reflects back."[22] *Light Body*, then, not only pictorializes a bodily phenomenon from Tibetan Buddhism but also renders

19. Carnes, *Beauty*, 214.

20. Dante, *Paradiso*, trans. Robert Hollander and Jean Hollander (New York, NY: Anchor, 2007), canto 33, lines 114–20.

21. As told to me in personal correspondence with Lia Chavez on February 8, 2017.

22. Gregory of Nyssa, "Letter 35 to Peter His Own Brother on the Divine Ousia and Hypostasis," in *Gregory of Nyssa: The Letters—Introduction, Translation, and Commentary*, trans. Anna M. Silvas (Leiden, Netherlands: Brill, 2007), 256.

the logic of the icon in the very media it employs—fleshly bodies and colored light. In this way, Chavez not only mirrors the light from her internal visions into her collaborative dance performance, but by doing so, she offers us an imaginative play on Dante's beatific vision. Consequentially, her triptych of intersecting rainbows in *Light Body* speaks not only to light's marvelous capacity for refraction but also to the body's iconic performativity in a triune God.

Pilar Timpane, *Women's March*, Washington, DC, 2017, digital photograph. Courtesy of the artist.

11 We Are Worldless Without One Another: An Interview with Judith Butler

by STEPHANIE BERBEC

*"We the people"—the utterance, the chant, the written line—
is always missing some group of people it claims to represent.*

—JUDITH BUTLER, *NOTES TOWARD
A PERFORMATIVE THEORY OF ASSEMBLY*

THE PHILOSOPHER AND GENDER theorist Judith Butler famously coined the term *gender performativity* in her 1990 book *Gender Trouble*. There, she posited the theory of gender, or the body, as one that acts and performs according to the conventions of gender, conventions that are influenced, from the start, before one is even born. Now, in her book *Notes Toward a Performative Theory of Assembly*, Butler uses gender performativity as a point of departure for discussing precarious populations and the assembly of bodies as protest. She interweaves her two theories of performativity and precarity with the works of Hannah Arendt, Giorgio Agamben, and Emmanuel Levinas as a way to critically assess and speak to Tahrir Square, Occupy, Black Lives Matter, and other movements of dissent. In this interview, we consider her work in light of the recent events at Standing Rock and the 2016 presidential election. When so many in our society today exist at the limits of recognizability, Butler writes from the perspective that there is no *I* without first a *we*, pushing against the current operative boundaries and toward a politics of alliance, cohabitation, and interdependency.

The Other Journal (TOJ): In your recent book, *Notes Toward a Performative Theory of Assembly*, you critically engage protest among the precarious as a sort of bodily performativity, making mention of the Occupy and Black Lives Matter movements, as well as other mass demonstrations around the world. Can you elaborate on why it makes sense to use gender performativity as a point of departure for talking about precarious communities and the assembly of bodies as a performative enactment?

Judith Butler (JB): I am sure that there are many ways to approach this problem. I suppose I was offering an intellectual itinerary for those readers who ask, how is it that you worked on gender and now work on violence, public demonstrations, and precarity? I do think that at stake in both forms of embodied performativity is a notion of political expression. Our political views are made known through speech and writing but also through images, sounds, and a wide range of artistic expression. Performance art is one such artistic practice with political consequences. It shows up in demonstrations, but can we also think of demonstrations as embodied forms of expression, ways of making political demands, even when speech is absent or not the salient form of expression?

TOJ: In a critique of identity politics you explain that it "fails to furnish a broader conception of what it means, politically, to live together, across differences, sometimes in modes of unchosen proximity, especially when living together, however difficult it may be, remains an ethical and political imperative."[1] I am thinking here about our reaction to the *impossible* outcome of this year's election and whether it has anything to do with the limitations of identity politics or the gap between discourse and practice. What does our shock tell us? In what ways have we missed the mark in our relations with the United States we thought we knew?

JB: That is a superb question that we will be asking for some time to come. Surely, the strong expressions of xenophobia and racism on the part of the Trump administration are signs that refugees and undocumented people—mainly figured as Syrians and Mexicans—are precisely *not* those with whom Trump and friends feel any obligation to live. In many ways, especially in its support of white supremacy, the Trump administration represents an attack on multiracial and multiethnic cohabitation. I think we have to ask how the partial popular support for closing the border with

---

1. Butler, *Notes Toward a Performative Theory of Assembly* (Cambridge, MA: Harvard University Press, 2015), 27.

a wall, discriminating against nations with large Muslim populations, and enacting deportation plans for the undocumented are linked with an increased sense of economic precarity and new forms of virulent racism. It may well be that those who voted for Trump were not always forthcoming with pollsters, understanding that racism and misogyny were unacceptable public discourse. At the same time, these shameful expressions were also clearly exhilarating for some who supported him. At last, they could throw off the superegoic control of feminist and antiracist discourse! We may have to think more about how shame and the exhilarations of unbridled hatred are linked and what political forms they assume. And it is true that we need to respond with a left project that does not simply line up the various identities whose rights we want to be secure. We have to ask what links us and what can link us to those who were too demoralized to vote or to those who thought that voting for Trump was the only way to say *no*. Many of those who voted for Trump did not know to what project they were saying *yes*. Some notion of who *we* are and can become now seems paramount—on what conditions do we live together, and what kinds of obligations bind us to one another and to the polities in which we live?

TOJ: You define *precarity* as a "politically induced condition in which certain populations suffer from failing social and economic networks of support more than others, and become differentially exposed to injury, violence, and death." What is key here, and what you've made clear throughout your text, is that precarity as a lived reality is not an individual condition. I am thinking here about the failures of religious institutions, specifically in their responsibility to protest on behalf of a whole host of persons—women, gender and sexual minorities, persons of color, refugees, immigrants, the undocumented, and those dispossessed of land—whose safety and well-being are now at risk of being compromised. In a stream of questions you ask "who will fail to be protected," and I think that is precisely the question that religious institutions need to be asking of themselves: who are *we* failing to protect?[2] An effort of solidarity demands a sharing in responsibility for the ways in which religious institutions have aided in keeping the precarious precarious. In light of its own genealogy of performative assemblages—and taking into consideration that many readers of *TOJ* are academic theologians, practitioners in the church, or studying to become one of the two—are there any collective and institutional ways the church might begin to address this?

JB: I have found it quite important that the current pope calls attention to poverty in many of his public statements. I am less sure how strongly that has translated into more support for antipoverty programs and for the support of refugee communities,

2. Ibid., 33 and 34.

but these are tasks in which religious institutions and networks remain essential. I am sorry, though, that the pope has chosen to continue the demonization of the term *gender* and the important feminist and LGBTQ movements that find that term essential for realizing their visions of social transformation and justice.

What may be most important right now, however, is to communicate the dignity of the religion of Islam, and to do whatever can be done to include Islam in interfaith networks and mobilizations. We know that every religion has its fundamentalists and that every religion can be demonized, which means that the rights of religious minorities must be protected, and *religious freedom* should not be abused as a principle to support those who seek to discriminate against gay, lesbian, trans, and gender nonconforming peoples. I worry that when we speak about so-called Western values, we too often presuppose that those are Judeo-Christian, and that implies that a wide range of religions are relegated outside the core values of Western society and even of humanity itself. This cannot be right.

TOJ: You encourage gender and sexual minorities to form links with other precarious communities, suggesting that precarity as a shared lived reality might operate as a site of alliance that joins people groups who otherwise have little in common. I am reminded here of the late anthropologist Victor Turner and his work on liminality and *communitas*. I think the concept of liminality may take this sort of relationality a bit further, as it cuts across even more categories, enabling alliances not only among the precarious but among the precarious and everyone else. If, as you've written, shared exposure can become the basis for resistance, and "we the people" is always enacting, always an "assembly of bodies, plural, persisting, acting, and laying claim to a public sphere by which one has been abandoned," what are your thoughts on the alliances that have formed and are continuing to form around the world postelection? And would you say that it is precisely within such a liminal space that we can most accurately say "we"?[3]

JB: I do think that we have to ask about the reasons that 23 percent of the voting public voted for Trump and to consider what extent strong feelings of demoralization and an increased sense of precarity led them to turn to a reactionary populist. Groups on the left now must make connections with two different kinds of people. On the one hand, if we have a better account of why so many people have been plunged into precarity and fear, then we have to make the case in terms that are popular and persuasive. On the other hand, we now have a burgeoning resistance movement of civil servants, state officials, and police departments who are refusing to implement deportation plans and travel bans. Those are our new allies. So in the moment when

---

3. Ibid., 38 and 59. Also see Turner, *The Ritual Process: Structure and Anti-Structure* (New Brunswick, NJ: Aldine Transaction, 1995).

we might want to retreat and find consolation among the like-minded, we need to reach out more effectively to persuade people that constitutional democracy and a common commitment to equality and freedom are goods worth fighting for and that cohabitation implies an affirmation of our ethnic and racial diversity as well as our religious diversity.

TOJ: That's fascinating. I am struck by your calling us to recognize those resisting state officials and police persons as our new allies. What might a common commitment to constitutional democracy, equality, and freedom look like in conjunction with these new allies? Particularly if some of those broader structures have a long history of policing and ensuring the suppression of those values?

JB: I am just aware that we are watching to see who among the Republicans still cares about the constitution or what it says. Or who among those people rallying at town halls in anger in the Midwest are making claims that the loss of health care is inhumane? My sense is that most populists aren't altogether clear about the source of their own anger, which means that it can be articulated in different political frames. In a sense, this is an opportunity.

TOJ: You make mention of the rise of the *sans papiers* or others within the "shadowy domain of existence" who, radically deprived of recognition, are beginning to enter into the sphere of appearance by way of mass demonstration, attempting to lay claim to space and demanding the right to appear, to say that their lives matter and that they exist. This brings to mind Maurice Merleau-Ponty's work of the body as a "gaping wound."[4] In this sense, protest, as bodily enactment and bodily vulnerability in the street or in the square, is essentially a visible exclamation and reminder that all is not well in the world. How might this conception mesh with your own in terms of how we think about the visible appearance of bodies in the public sphere? And what's made available to us or overlooked here as we seek language that may aid in the destigmatization of fear that is associated with a large group of bodies assembled and the misconstrual of protest as innately violent?

JB: I am sure that Merleau-Ponty is in the background of my thoughts, for he is the one who tells us that the limits of the body do not contain us but expose us to a world without which our living is not possible. Indeed, we are given over from the start, so to have a body is already to be in the care of the other or to be in need of such care.

---

4. Butler, *Notes Toward a Performative Theory of Assembly*, 41 and 198; and Merleau-Ponty, *Phenomenology of Perception*, trans. C. Smith (London, UK: Routledge and Kegan Paul, 1978), quoted in Mark C. Taylor, *Altarity* (Chicago, IL: University of Chicago Press, 1987), 69.

We cannot separate our idea of a persisting body from networks of care in this regard; when infrastructures fail and falter, so too do we.

I am open to a world that acts on me in ways that cannot be fully predicted or controlled in advance, and something about my openness is not, strictly speaking, under my control. That opening toward the world is not something that I can exactly will away. This social character of our persistence and our possible flourishing means that we have to take collective responsibility for overcoming conditions of induced precarity. Demonstrations that oppose evictions in Barcelona and demonstrations that oppose police brutality against black men and women in the United States are making claims of justice; they are documenting the failures of justice, and they are part of our political freedom and even our political hope. I see how often those demonstrations are called "riots" or "unrest" and how quickly they can be shut down for reasons of "security." But without the freedom of movement and assembly, we lose our very character as a democracy.

I was in a cab the other day in New York City passing a demonstration against Trump on West Fourth Street. I said to Oscar, the cab driver, "They will be there every week." He responded, "And then they will be there every day and every night," at which point I was reminded how revolutionary movements for social justice emerge.

TOJ: In processing the recent events at Standing Rock, I was struck by the words you share of the black American feminist Bernice Johnson Reagon, "that interdependency includes the threat of death."[5] To what extent are interdependency, cohabitation, alliance, and the power of assembly being properly demonstrated with veterans joining the front lines on behalf of water protectors at Standing Rock, particularly in the joining of two different sets of "disposable persons"?

JB: The veterans arriving at Standing Rock is moving indeed. This kind of alliance is beautiful because the veterans were able to depart from a nationalist and militarist affiliation, and because the native peoples and their allies were able to welcome them. That the veterans now stand off against the militarized police force tasked with dispersing the demonstrators makes plain that there are fissures developing that may well make it more possible for police and members of the National Guard to refuse to implement orders to deport, detain, and disperse precarious peoples seeking to lay claim to land, freedom, equality, and belonging. That the Los Angeles Police Department also made clear it will not implement any deportation policy shows us that new alliances are possible, ones that are even more queer than those we have already known.

---

5. Johnson Reagon quoted in Butler, *Notes Toward a Performative Theory of Assembly*, 152.

TOJ: You critically engage the work of Hannah Arendt in this text, specifically her book *The Human Condition*. Although there are several instances in which you depart from or expand upon her work, you agree with Arendt's notion that freedom "does not come from me or from you; it can and does happen as a relation *between* us, or, indeed, among us" and that together "we bring the space of appearance into being."[6] This idea of the *between* occurs so often throughout your text, and perhaps just as often, there are mentions of this sort of juxtaposition between being bound to the other and coming undone in the presence of the other. Can you explain your view of what occurs in the *between* of two subjects in relation, the boundedness and the coming undone, as well as the ways in which this becomes the space for freedom?

JB: I think that Arendt was right to criticize those forms of individualism that presume that freedom is always and only a matter of personal liberty. Of course, I am most glad to have my personal liberty, but I only have it to the extent that there is a sphere of freedom in which I can operate. That sphere is coproduced by people who live together or who have agreed to live in a world in which the relations between them make possible their individual sense of being free. So perhaps we might regard personal liberty as a cipher of social freedom. And social freedom cannot be understood apart from what arises between people, what happens when they make something in common or when, in fact, they seek to make or remake the world in common. I am struck by the way Arendt's position echoes that of Martin Buber, whose cultural Zionism interested her a great deal in the 1930s. For Buber, the *I* only knows its world because there is a *you* who has consciousness of that world.[7] The world is given to me because you are also there as one to whom it is given. The world is never given to me alone but always in your company. Without you, the world does not give itself. We are worldless without one another.

TOJ: The third chapter opens by asking "whether any of us have the capacity or inclination to respond ethically to suffering at a distance, and what makes that ethical encounter possible when it does take place?"[8] I am wondering whether the question here is not between "capacity *or* inclination" (emphasis added); that is, not a matter of whether we all have the capacity to respond but that few of us are inclined to actually do so. It seems we have an operative, perhaps even subconscious, mentality that we have less of an ethical obligation to those from whom the distance from us is great. What is this seeming disconnect between our capacity to respond to the suffering other and our inclination to actually do so?

6. Arendt quoted in Butler, *Notes Toward a Performative Theory of Assembly*, 89 (emphasis added).
7. See Buber, *I and Thou* (New York, NY: Simon and Schuster, 1971).
8. Butler, *Notes Toward a Performative Theory of Assembly*, 99.

JB: I think you are probably right. What worries me is that many of us form our sense of obligation toward another on the basis of feelings of identification. If someone else is like us, and that likeness is readily recognizable, then we are more inclined to respond in the way that we would have others respond to us. The harder task is to maintain an obligation to those by whom we feel ourselves to have been injured, to those we fear, or to those whose difference from us seems to be quite severe. This is why I do not think that global obligations can rest on identification, even expanded or expanding identifications; they have to claim us quite regardless of whether or not we feel love or sympathy, for the simple reason that the world is given to us in common and that without each other the world is not given. If the self is the basis of sympathy, our sympathy will be restricted to those who are like us. The real challenge occurs when that extrapolation of the self is thwarted by alterity.

TOJ: It does seem that any way forward must include maintaining an obligation to those we perceive to have hurt us or to those whom we fear, but current conservative critiques of political correctness seem to pose such obligations or lines of connection to others as illusions. How do we foster obligation in a time such as this?

JB: That is a good question, and I am not sure I have the answer. But it does matter when one starts to realize that one's own suffering is like that of the other's. That can lead to a structural understanding of exploitation or differential precarity. Some forms of identification or substitutability can begin forms of alliance that call into question the more entrenched versions of individualism. The idea that I am obligated to others follows, I think, from the more fundamental insight that one life is not living without the other and that this way of being bound up together is at once ontological and ethical.

TOJ: This brings to mind the Jewish and Christian notion of neighbor. We want a definable answer to the *who* implicit in the injunction to love our neighbor because already there are those whom we wish to exclude. Stepping outside of the general binaries through which we view our complex world, often to our own detriment, I'm thinking here about the theory of neighbor as a third term coupled with the idea of proximity, the root of which means *nearest*.[9] Could it be suggested that the neighbor, as neither friend nor enemy, is perhaps *always* in proximity, always nearest, always present, but neither fully and finally friend or enemy, never arriving but always remaining something other? To be more specific, if we understand proximity to be the space within which interpersonal relations occur, the breeding ground for contempt, as well as the site for ethical obligation, could our conception of proximity

---

9. See Kenneth Reinhard, "Toward a Political Theology of the Neighbor," in *The Neighbor: Three Inquiries in Political Theology* (Chicago, IL: University of Chicago Press, 2005), 13.

be expanded, albeit metaphysically, to include our geographically distant neighbors, such that it could be suggested that we *always* have an obligation to the other, even at a distance?

JB: I like this idea, of course, but sometimes the greatest estrangement happens within relations that are most proximate. I am interested in the fact, for instance, that many people claim that they follow principles of nonviolence except that they would make exceptions if someone in their family were attacked or threatened. That suggests that those lives closest to us are most precious and that others are less so. Yet most violence takes place within domestic situations, suggesting that those closest to us also represent distinct sorts of threats. There seems to be no way around that paradox. We let others die because they are far away, but those closest to us are sometimes most imperiled by proximity. Violence works across proximity and distance, it seems.

TOJ: You advocate an ethics of cohabitation, bluntly reminding us that it is "not from a pervasive love for humanity or a pure desire for peace that we strive to live together. We live together because we have no choice." In fact, you point out that we don't even get to choose with whom we cohabit and that interdependency does not mean social harmony.[10] What are the implications for such given realities when the work we have before us necessitates the linking of bodies, the forming of alliances, and the performativity of assemblies?

JB: Very often those links we make are anonymous. We do not know the history or the face of the one with whom we are allied. This is part of what makes it a public demonstration rather than the local assertion of community bonds. Sometimes those two sorts of ties are mixed. There has to be a way of entering into a common world, especially for those who have not been part of that world, to ally with those who are at risk of not counting. This means that we do not demand a personal connection or even an alliance of affect but a passionate commitment to the everyone and the anyone. Maybe there are forms of love that can describe this, but they would be neither personal nor communitarian.

TOJ: In this recent text, you seem comfortable with a mode of public writing and speaking that does not directly or immediately lead to action; you even mention the urgency with which you write so that your work might first cause us to pause and reflect together on the very conditions of acting.[11] What's made available to us in such forms of reflection that we might otherwise miss when we become too preoccupied with immediate actionable steps?

10. Butler, *Notes Toward a Performative Theory of Assembly*, 122. Also see 121 and 151.
11. Ibid., 124.

JB: I see on my campus, for instance, that there are students who oppose racism by any means necessary. I want to oppose racism as well, but I do think it is worth pausing to ask by what means. If the means are violent, how are they justified? I would like to persuade people who are in righteous rage that the turn to violence is not what they finally want, since at stake is not just finding a way to react immediately and legibly but building a world together. We have to pause and ask about means if we want to build a world opposed to racism.

TOJ: In your acceptance speech for the Adorno award, which is included at the end of the book, you pick up Adorno's question on the possibility of living a good life in a bad life. You argue that whatever hope we have for a good life in this troubled historical moment and context is bound up with interdependency and performative action. You write, "If I am to lead a good life, it will be a life lived with others, a life that is no life without those others."[12] I am struck by the ways in which you hold together the tensions involved in answering Adorno's question—being honest about our present moment while also remaining hopeful about our possibilities in collective action. What is it that gives you hope for us moving toward a good life in this moment?

JB: I suppose at this moment I am most grateful for the moments of surprise; the alliance between the veterans and the Standing Rock activists; the people who take to the street to oppose the travel ban; the law students who stay up all night helping to draft the rationale for denying that ban; the farmers, many of whom are Republicans, who do not want migrant workers deported or living in fear of a police raid. There are many of us coming together to ask our universities to become sanctuaries, which means we will in no way assist state authorities in their efforts to deport undocumented students. Many of these people I do not know. Many people meet each other for the first time. Many are surprised to find solidarity in a sector long regarded as culturally alien. So I am moved by the alliances and think that they can grow into a popular movement but only if we do not know in advance with whom we will be allying. We need that opening to a different alliance in the future to affirm hope. I see some discrete moments, vibrant and compelling, and hope to see the coming concatenation soon.

TOJ: It seems like this sort of surprise may necessarily stay hidden from view until we actually cast our lots into the movement to build a world together, as you say. Do actionable steps only become possible or imaginable in the wake of interconnection, of thinking alongside this other with whom I have nothing in common apart from our commitment to a sharable, equitable future?

12. Ibid., 218.

JB: I suppose it is first important to honor the obligation to affirm the life of another even if I am overwhelmed with hostility. This is the basic precept of an ethics of nonviolence, in my view. So though we imagine that we throw our lot in with others, the fact is that others are impinging upon us all the time. We were thrown into a world of others way before we made any decisions whether or not to throw our lot in with others. Decision only happens in the context of a prior entanglement. That can be a tie of ambivalence, but it is a social tie or bond, one that is sometimes nearly impossible to fathom. And that we are all equally in that bind, as it were, implies a kind of equality from the start. We can rebel against it, but the truth of that sort of equality is larger than our rebellion. The point is to take that non-egological point of departure for what we call our agency and our decision. It means that action is always implicitly plural and reciprocal, even when that is not the case in existing circumstances. We have to foreground and *work* that incommensurability to produce a different future.

12 Behind Blue Eyes: Consubstantiality and the Unthinkable

by RUSSELL JOHNSON

WHITE.
Male.
Twenties.
Over six feet tall.
Short, brown hair.
Medium build.

This is a description of me. It is also a description of Timothy McVeigh, who on April 19, 1995, planted a bomb inside a federal building in Oklahoma City, killing 168 people.

McVeigh and I both grew up in the northeast, reading comic books, watching football, and doing well in school. Our pasts are similar; our bodies are similar. So what makes him different from me? Maybe it's his eyes. My eyes are green; his eyes are a piercing blue. Look at his eyes, and you will see we're not the same.

I find it unsettling to think that my body and Timothy McVeigh's body have so much in common. I do not like to dwell on the fact that he and I are the same species. And so I find some solace in the fact that the first biography published about him is titled *All-American Monster*. If I am a human and he is a monster, I do not have to wrestle with the notion that he and I are made of the same stuff. We may look similar—except for those eyes—but inside he must be a different being altogether, inhuman and terrifying. We may have the same skin, but rest assured, our similarities are only skin deep.

To borrow a term from the rhetorical theorist Kenneth Burke, I feel compelled to deny my *consubstantiality* with McVeigh. For Burke, rhetoric works not so much through persuasion as through identification. Rhetoric has the power to create, sustain, modify, and reject identifications—this is like that, I am like you, they are not like us. According to Burke, the main purpose of language in human life is establishing consubstantiality. He writes, "In being identified with B, A is 'substantially one' with a person other than himself. Yet at the same time, he remains unique, an individual locus of motives. Thus he is both joined and separate, at once a distinct substance and consubstantial with another."[1]

We see the work of rhetoric establishing consubstantiality in the wake of tragedy. "We are all Trayvon Martin," signs read. "Je suis Charlie," millions tweeted. Black men wear "I am Mike Brown" hoodies while across the world women chant "I am Malala." People rush to identify themselves with the victims, sometimes out of solidarity, sometimes out of slacktivism, sometimes out of fear, sometimes as a way to remember the fallen—"re-member" literally meaning to re-embody, to make consubstantial with.[2]

Sometimes this identification is used to demonstrate the similarity between victims and protestors. A young black man wearing an "I am Trayvon" hoodie is a walking reminder of arbitrary violence against blacks and the way such violence is permitted by our justice system. That hoodie communicates the message, "Look at my body—under different circumstances, that could have been me."

This brings me to the question at the heart of this paper. Should I wear an "I am Timothy McVeigh" shirt? Look at my body—under different circumstances, that could have been me. What should I do when I recognize my consubstantiality—not with a victim but with a murderer?

This is not a question white people are accustomed to asking. The American white majority has a simple but effective strategy to deny consubstantiality with murderers. If a killer has an Arab body, then many of us assume he is a terrorist whose actions are motivated by Islamic fundamentalism. His motives, we immediately conclude, are not just different from our potential motives for violence; they are of an entirely different nature. We disidentify, locating the source of the terrorist's actions

---

1. Burke, *Rhetoric of Motives* (Berkeley, CA: University of California Press, 1969), 21.

2. *Slacktivism* is a term for someone who signals (often on social media) their support for a cause but does not actually do anything to help that cause. The term goes back to at least 1995.

in something totally foreign to us. It is not an exaggeration to say that we characterize the terrorist as a different species from us, a creature driven by forces we cannot feel.

If a killer has a black body, we assume the violence is gang-related. We disidentify by contextualizing the violence as a part of a lifestyle that is utterly separate from our own, a lifestyle of crime. The word *criminal*, like the word *terrorist*, designates a different species in the dominant white imagination, and it is as racially coded as the phrase *bad neighborhood*. Whereas a word like *felon* designates a person who has committed a crime, the word *criminal* designates a kind of being wholly other from us law-abiding citizens.[3] Black violence is not the work of someone consubstantial with us; it is the work of a criminal. Furthermore, this disidentification is used to justify violence against innocent blacks. Consider how many blacks have been arrested or killed because they "matched a description," because they were consubstantial with criminals. For police-shooting victim Philando Castile, it was not his eyes but his "wide-set nose" that was enough to separate him from the law-abiding world.[4]

When a killer has a white body, we assume that he is mentally ill. This, too, is a way of denying consubstantiality. "Sure, our bodies are superficially alike," we think, "but he's nothing like me—he's insane." This appeal to mental health in the wake of mass shootings is not an attempt to explain anything but rather to explain away our consubstantiality, to dismiss the need for explanation.

There are some instances in which Arab violence is an act of terrorism, black violence is gang-related, and white violence arises from mental illness, but when a new tragedy occurs, these precedents do not fully explain our instinct to diagnose the event in this way before all of the facts are revealed.[5] Our instinctive judgments, the way we know what happened before we really know what happened, come from a felt need to deny our own consubstantiality with the perpetrators. This is a felt need to distance and excuse ourselves and to reassure ourselves that *they* are evil but *we* are good. Even when mass violence makes us feel less secure in our schools and workplaces, these instinctive judgments help us feel more secure in our identities, more secure in our bodies.

Should Timothy McVeigh make me feel insecure? He persistently evades all attempts to deny consubstantiality. For starters, he had no connections to any terrorist

---

3. This is the process of *pseudo-speciation*, an idea first described by Erik Erikson and explained in greater depth by Irenäus Eibl-Eibesfeldt.

4. Angela Bronner Helm, "Report: Philando Castile Was Pulled Over Because He Matched Description of Suspect with 'Wide-Set Nose,'" *Root*, July 10, 2016, http://www.theroot.com/articles/news/2016/07/philando-castile-pulled-over-because-he-matched-description-of-suspect-with-wide-set-nose-shots-fired-less-than-2-minutes-later/.

5. The frequency that Arab violence is terrorism, black violence is gang-related, and white violence stems from mental illness is far less than one might suspect. Consider for example the statistics in "Don't Blame Mental Illness for Gun Violence," *New York Times*, December 15, 2015, http://www.nytimes.com/2015/12/16/opinion/dont-blame-mental-illness-for-gun-violence.html.

organizations, though some have concocted a wild story about his role as the fall guy for a Philippine terrorist group. Indeed, McVeigh's own defense lawyer heard McVeigh's confession and still insisted that there had to be an international conspiracy behind the bombing. McVeigh was not previously a criminal—quite the opposite, in fact. He had worked for years as a security guard and had won five medals for his military service in the Gulf War. He had what his biographers later called a "squeaky-clean record."[6]

Nor was Timothy McVeigh mentally ill, though everyone assumed so in the initial media storm that followed the bombings.[7] Over a five-week period in prison, he went through twenty-five hours of interviews with a psychiatrist who reported that McVeigh was surprisingly normal, a "nice guy" with "no major mental illness" who was not delusional and fully understood what he had done. McVeigh's lawyer argued that the bombing "was not a sadistic crime, like the bloody murder sprees of Charles Manson or John Wayne Gacy. . . . He is not a demon, though surely his act was demonic."[8] Those who spent time with McVeigh all seem to agree. McVeigh is not a demon; he is a nice guy. He is not one of them; he is one of us.

What needs to be stressed here is that the psychiatrist, lawyer, and biographers are not wrong about McVeigh. They are not in denial about his personality; they are not softening his image or distorting the truth to make it more palatable. If anything, they are making the truth far more unsettling because we desperately want McVeigh to be a demon. He would be so much easier to deal with if his eyes were red, not blue.

McVeigh did not act like a madman; he acted like an American. In his mind, the bombing was a "counter-attack" against a US government that had declared war on its own people in the massacres at Waco and Ruby Ridge. The government had become oppressive, and a demonstration of power needed to be made to check its

6. For McVeigh's record and his lawyer's alternate explanations for the bombing ("At various times [Stephen] Jones tried to link the bombing to associates of Terry Nichols in the Philippines; to Osama bin Laden and other Arab terrorists; to a German descendent of a Nazi Party leader; to neo-Nazis in Great Britain; to Ramzi Yousef, mastermind of the World Trade Center bombing; and to associates of a white separatist group in the Oklahoma compound Elohim City"), see Lou Michel and Dan Herbeck, *American Terrorist: Timothy McVeigh and the Oklahoma City Bombing* (New York, NY: HarperCollins, 2001), 286 and 372. Note that Jones's explanations were not simply a legal strategy; he has persisted in his attempt to link McVeigh to international terrorist groups even after the trial was over, as have many others; see Jones, *Others Unknown: The Oklahoma City Bombing Case and Conspiracy* (New York, NY: Public Affairs, 2001).

7. Reflecting on the media coverage of the McVeigh case, Gore Vidal writes, "The media had so quickly and thoroughly attributed his crime to that stock American villain, the lone crazed killer" (Vidal, *Perpetual War for Perpetual Peace* [New York City, NY: Thunder's Mouth Press/Nation Books, 2002], 46; see also ix). Note also that mental health professionals do not think simply in terms of ill and not ill; thus, here and elsewhere my terminology and descriptions of mental illness reflect the ways these terms function in the American public imagination rather than as nuanced, clinical approaches to mental health.

8. Michel and Herbeck, *American Terrorist*, 290 and 345 (cf. Robin Aitken, "Inside McVeigh's Mind," *BBC News*, June 11, 2001, http://news.bbc.co.uk/2/hi/americas/1382540.stm; and Vidal, *Perpetual War*, 103.

militancy. He decided to use the American government's own tactics against it.[9] As McVeigh said, "borrowing a page from US foreign policy, I decided to send a message to a government that was becoming increasingly hostile, by bombing a government building and the government employees within that building who represent that government. Bombing the Murrah Federal Building was morally and strategically equivalent to the United States hitting a government building in Serbia, Iraq, or other nations." McVeigh argued that it was hypocritical for the federal government to call him monstrous for killing children as "collateral damage" because that very same government ordered the death of many children in military strikes and domestic operations. "Whether you wish to admit it or not," McVeigh wrote, "when you approve, morally, of the bombing of foreign targets by the US military, you are approving of acts morally equivalent to the bombing in Oklahoma City." He saw his actions as parallel to the bombings of Hiroshima and Nagasaki—they were violent but for the sake of a greater peace and a greater freedom. "The end," as he said, "outweighs the means."[10]

I want to stop for a moment and acknowledge a temptation. I could end this essay here and have McVeigh's harrowing evaluation of American foreign policy be the final point. But to do so would be to deny consubstantiality with McVeigh. All too often pacifism, or even a broader Christian social justice identification, serves as a way of disidentifying with aggressors. To rest secure in a perspective that characterizes us as peaceful and aggressors as violent is to refuse to follow the God who was crucified between two criminals. In a bodily way, Christ identified with these violent men. Only in this final act of consubstantiality was the incarnation complete. God did not just become of one substance with law-abiding citizens but with criminals, refusing even at the final moment to deny consubstantiality with murderers.

If we refuse to acknowledge what we have in common with others, we shut ourselves off, not only from understanding them but from understanding ourselves. When we deny consubstantiality, we refuse to admit that the other sheds any light on who or what we are. McVeigh compared his actions to those of a victim standing up to a bully. "Once you bloody the bully's nose," he said, "and he knows he's going to get punched again, he's not coming back around." That does not sound like the twisted logic of a terrorist, a criminal, or a madman. It sounds unsettlingly reasonable. When asked by a friend about all the people killed in the bombing, McVeigh replied, "Think about the people as if they were storm troopers in *Star Wars*. They may

---

9. The term *counter-attack* is McVeigh's; cf. Vidal, *Perpetual War*, 98f. His use of what he calls American government tactics in this counterattack is shown in Michel and Herbeck, *American Terrorist*, 169.

10. McVeigh, "McVeigh's letter to Rita Cosby," *Independence.net*, April 27, 2001, http://independence.net/okc/mcveighletterfox.htm; McVeigh, "An Essay on Hypocrisy," *Outpost of Freedom*, March 1998, http://www.outpost-of-freedom.com/mcveigh/okcaug98.htm; and McVeigh quoted in Michel and Herbeck, *American Terrorist*, 166.

be individually innocent, but they are guilty because they work for the Evil Empire."[11] I am unnerved by how much sense that makes to me. I am not Timothy McVeigh, but he and I are not so different. The process of reckoning with that fact is the process of coming to understand myself. This self-understanding makes me uncomfortable because it forces me to confront the ways I am not loving my neighbor. It forces me to see continuities between my own actions and those actions I disidentify with, the actions of a "them."

Acknowledging our consubstantiality with murderers is a challenge for all people, but it is especially difficult for white Americans who, as I mentioned earlier, have an array of subconscious strategies to help them disidentify with those who do evil acts. We automatically situate the source of evil actions in motivations that are utterly foreign to us, and by doing so we insulate ourselves from moral interrogation. We repress the possibility that acts of terrible violence emerge from urges, fears, or commitments that we share. This refusal to acknowledge consubstantiality reinforces a collective self-deception. Unable to understand ourselves or our neighbors, we find it difficult to truly love either.

Consubstantiality is often wrongly interpreted as guilt. I am not guilty of McVeigh's crime. I am not guilty of the evil of chattel slavery or the sins of Jim Crow racism or of the murders of innocent black men by police officers. And as I understand them, contemporary civil rights writers and activists do not want me to feel guilty for those evils. Rather, their challenge to white Americans is to recognize that we are of one substance with perpetrators of great evil, both in the past and the present. White guilt is a red herring. What is needed instead is to face the fact that people with bodies like mine have committed injustices and to let that fact call into question my own actions and motivations. The task of white theology in America is forming people capable of resisting the temptation to deny consubstantiality with victims and victimizers.

Timothy McVeigh was executed on June 11, 2001. He died with his eyes open, staring at those who were watching his execution.[12] The crucified Jesus beckons me to look into those blue eyes and see my own reflection. Jesus calls me, calls us all, to resist the pharisaical urge to say "God, I thank thee that I am not like other men" and to say instead, "Have mercy on us."[13]

---

11. Quoted in Michel and Herbeck, *American Terrorist*, 383 and 166 (cf. 224–25).

12. There was a two-way mirror separating McVeigh from the small crowd gathered for the execution. McVeigh directed his gaze at that mirror and also stared into the camera.

13. See Luke 18:11–12.

13 Jesus Doesn't Want Me for a Sunbeam: Thoughts on Depression, Race, and Theology

by PETER HERMAN

"SUCCESS AS THEOLOGIANS, PASTORS, and graduate students of theology must be secondary to the goal of loving God and neighbor, the weak and helpless of the land"—I encountered these words from James Cone as a first-semester graduate student at Union Theological Seminary in New York.[1] They left an indelible impression on me. It is an impression I have sometimes been at odds to understand.

Later in the same speech, Cone expounded on Paul, noting that "God chose what was foolish in order to put shame to the world's wise. What the world counts as base and despises, even the things that did not exist, God chose. Why? That God might do away with that which does exist."[2] This is a compelling theology for all of Christianity—it turns upside down the priorities of the world. The world loves power and exploitation. The world hates a loser. In Jesus, especially in Cone's understanding, the world is shown the foolishness of brute power, and our hopes are carried with Jesus not to die on the cross but to survive beyond it and be transformed. This should be vindicating or comforting for the oppressed. It is, however, paradoxical for those of us who groan beneath the yoke of depression: when suffering from depression, we are among the base and despised, yet we are unable to feel the warmth of God's

---

1. Cone, "The Vocation of a Theologian," *Union News* (Winter 1991): 4.
2. Ibid.

preferential choice. When I feel that my own brain is trying to kill me, that my wife cannot possibly love me, or that my son will reject me when he is old enough to realize what a nonperson I truly am, there is little comfort in Cone's words about God's love for the lowly. Nevertheless, my experience of nonpersonhood—of nonbeing—has forced me to develop an empathetic connection to others. It has led me to an awareness of my kinship with the very people whom Cone speaks of as the "oppressed of the land." Because of my depression, I now have a limited understanding of what it means to be told by white men that one is not a person worthy of consideration. I can begin to understand this because that is what I have been told by a white man, because that is what I have told myself.

The paradoxical message that emerges from Cone's reflection strikes me hard when reading the words of Jesus. Take, for example, his words from the cross about self-denial. In Mark's version, we have the following:

> He called the crowd with his disciples, and said to them, "If any want to become my followers, let them deny themselves and take up their cross and follow me. For those who want to save their life will lose it, and those who lose their life for my sake, and for the sake of the gospel, will save it. For what will it profit them to gain the whole world and forfeit their life?'" (8:34–37 NRSV).

This passage, as well as its parallels in Luke and John, is often interpreted to mean that we must be willing to forgo luxuries and worldly approval in order to be genuine disciples of Christ. The crosses that we are to take up represent our individual burdens, which are often interpreted as the burden of our own past sins. In my depression, however, I read a very different suggestion in this text.

The cross isn't something to be borne during my life—life *is* the cross. The act of being alive—breathing, eating, speaking with others—is a burden. I don't want to save my life; my life is my cross. Even though I know that there is a world of difference between martyrdom and suicide, I find myself wondering whether Mark's Jesus is letting me know that it might be OK to let go of that cross. After all, I suffer by living, and Jesus promises to end suffering, doesn't he? This question suggests a somewhat unorthodox reading of these texts—a hermeneutics of suicide is not listed in theology textbooks or preached from the Sunday pulpit. Yet this theological perspective has marked my twenty-five-year struggle with major depressive disorder.

These days, ideas of suicide come and go, but thanks to the efforts of a good therapist and a good prescriber such thoughts are largely a nattering buzz, a nuisance. But this has not always been the case. Such thoughts have, in my recent past, been more insistent. They have been more plausible and credible than I like to admit. In the quiet hours of the day, there is an inaudible yet persistent voice that answers Jesus's suggestion that I must hate life itself with "Yes, I do hate life. I hate it so much. Life itself *is* my cross. Let me lay it down, Lord. Please, let me lay it down." I argue back against this urge. I resist. I rationalize. I take the pills. I go to the sessions. And then that internal monologue is quieter, but it's still there. I doubt it will ever be silent.

When my depression is heightened and my internal struggle especially fraught, my hermeneutic of suicide dominates my encounters with Scripture. My studies in theology have taught me that Jesus's sayings about self-denial are metaphorical and that church teaching is strikingly consistent in its criticism of suicide, yet these facts don't easily loosen the existential hold of suicidal thinking on my psyche. And so, rather than dismissing the scriptural interpretations that have arisen from suicidal thinking, I have found that they can illuminate otherwise overlooked truths in Scripture that have profoundly affected my Christian life for the better.

Consider, for instance, the story of the Gerasene demoniac, a healing/exorcism story with a strong thematic connection to mental illness:

> They came to the other side of the sea, to the country of the Gerasenes. And when he had stepped out of the boat, immediately a man out of the tombs with an unclean spirit met him. He lived among the tombs; and no one could restrain him any more, even with a chain; for he had often been restrained with shackles and chains, but the chains he wrenched apart, and the shackles he broke in pieces; and no one had the strength to subdue him. Night and day among the tombs and on the mountains he was always howling and bruising himself with stones. When he saw Jesus from a distance, he ran and bowed down before him; and he shouted at the top of his voice, "What have you to do with me, Jesus, Son of the Most High God? I adjure you by your God, do not torment me." For he had said to him "Come out of the man, you unclean spirit!" Then Jesus asked him "What is your name?" He replied "My name is Legion; for we are many." (Mark 5:1–9)

R. S. Sugirtharajah considers this passage from the context of postcolonialism, noting the colonized context from which the authors of Mark approach the text. From this perspective, he treats "the action of Jesus as neutering the only option the oppressed people had in declaring their opposition to the colonial occupation."[3] For Sugurtharajah, feigning "madness," or even legitimately succumbing to it as an effect of posttraumatic stress disorder, was and is a method of nonviolent resistance to a colonial oppressor. The demoniac is noted for his strength—neither chains nor shackles could hold him—and likely would have been conscripted into the Roman legions. By

---

3. Sugirtharajah, *Postcolonial Criticism and Biblical Interpretation* (New York, NY: Oxford University Press, 2002), 94.

removing the demons, Sugurtharajah suggests, Jesus may have prevented this man from resisting his oppressor.

Depression has often positioned me in the place of the demoniac, filled with the "unclean spirits" of depressive and suicidal thoughts. In this state, I've wondered, as Sugurtharajah does, whether it would be better to have my tormenting spirits driven off a cliff or to live in the tombs as an outcast. I am frighteningly uncertain about whether the exorcism of my depression would be good or bad. There are days that I wish for those spirits to be gone, and there are days that I feel so bound to something I know to be toxic that I cannot imagine myself without this illness. There is, in other words, a kind of ontological codependence between the healed person I wish to be and the unhealable wretch I fear that I actually am. The tension implicit in this relationship determines my reading, not only for the fifth chapter of Mark but also more broadly for theology as a discipline.

Indeed, my depression has shaped my work as a theologian with insights that I would not possess were I miraculously healed of this condition. First, depression offers me an empathetic point of entry to understanding black experience, especially in the work of James Cone, whose work is central to my own. To be sure, I do not intend to suggest equivalence between my suffering as a white man with depression and the suffering of a black woman or man who struggles to have her or his humanity recognized. They are not the same thing. Depression or no, I still receive the benefits of whiteness in a society that tilts toward unjust idolatry of the white body.

Yet I still see myself reflected in the writing of Cone. In his memoir *My Soul Looks Back*, Cone recounts the following about his boyhood community: "God was that reality to which the people turned for identity and worth because the existing social, political, and economic structures said that they were nobody."[4] I am a beneficiary of those same social, political, and economic structures that told the black citizens of Bearden, Arkansas, they were nobody. Yet I also struggle daily with an internal narrator who tells me that I am nobody. In other words, I find it easy to believe that black people can be held down by the white man saying they are worthless because I also have a white man telling me I am worthless, because I also feel the weight and difficulty of rising up from under that ever-present critique. I do not have access to the internal life of someone like Cone, a black man raised in the apartheid South, but I can understand the horrible tension that arises between a religious life that says "you are valued and cherished" and a world that says "you are worthless and disposable." I can appreciate with the oppressed that the latter statement is a distortion of reality while also understanding that the affective impact of that statement is not dulled merely by recognizing it as false.

In the 1970 foreword to *A Black Theology of Liberation*, Cone states that,

---

4. Cone, *My Soul Looks Back* (Maryknoll, NY: Orbis, 1986), 23.

> There will be no peace in America until whites begin to hate their whiteness, asking from the depths of their being: "How can we become black?"... But until then, it is the task of the Christian theologian to do theology in the light of the concreteness of human oppression as expressed in color, and to interpret for the oppressed the meaning of God's liberation in their community.[5]

Cone's call to hate my whiteness gives structure to Jesus's declaration that unless I hate life itself, I cannot be a disciple. Cone does not mean that we must hate our white skin or our white bodies but that we should hate the oppression and exclusion they have come to signify in our society; we should hate the sociopolitical framework that values the supremacy of one skin color above all others.

Cone offers me a framework that can counter the suicidal hatred of life-as-continued-metabolism which I might otherwise hear in Jesus's words. It is not living that is detestable and must end. It is living as white. It is accepting unearned privilege as valid and deserved. It is my passive continuation of a system of white supremacy that values my life and my being more than Cone's simply because of the accidents of our biographies.

The experience of depression and suicidal thinking has thus left me with an opening to experience something of the tension Cone discusses, to experience something of a society that says no to what God, in Jesus, affirms, namely, our own worth and humanity. Contrary to Cone's context of external political and social struggle, this is an internal struggle on my part. Nobody else is telling me that I am unworthy of God's love. I'm left in a state of uneasy worry. I question God's wisdom and knowledge, asking, "How can God believe that I am a person worthy of existence and salvation, when I know in my bones that this is not the case?" There is no easy answer, but I do know that this worry and doubt shape my theological context. I read healing stories of the Gospels and wonder what "healing" really means. I can empathize, even slightly, with the lament of Cone's theology. Perhaps I can speak to others in my sociopolitical context to let them know: James Cone is right. Jesus doesn't need white Christians.

In this way, my depression has connected me to larger interests of justice and community. Depression affords me a connection to the contexts of Sugirtharajah and Cone, which in turn help me see more to the sayings of Jesus that we've already examined. Their readings then add new dimension to my depressive hermeneutic. When I view myself as the demoniac and Legion as the internalized structures of whiteness, I can fully agree that the racist bias that takes hold of me should be cast into a herd of swine or into the sea. This is a justice-oriented identification with the text that my suicidal hermeneutic alone cannot afford. According to this reading, Jesus does not

---

5. Cone, *A Black Theology of Liberation*, 20th Anniversary Edition (Maryknoll, NY: Orbis, 1986), v–vi.

heal me as just one individual. The exorcism of white supremacy must unfold as a communal healing.

But I must also attend to Sugirtharajah's less-charitable reading of the story. It is still possible that the presence of Jesus can be used to pacify troublemakers and bend resisters to the will of an oppressive social regime. One needn't look further than the white TV evangelists and megachurches or practitioners of the so-called prosperity gospel to see how this might work out. The Jesus who calls us to fellowship too soon is the one who can reply "All Lives Matter" to the calls that "Black Lives Matter." Christians who follow the Jesus who calls for unity above all can overlook the dangers faced by marginalized people under Donald Trump's presidency, assenting to a cynical call to unity that demands no sacrifice on their part. Whatever else Jesus does in the Gospels, he calls us to change. All Christians struggle to determine what Christian transformation looks like. This is particularly tricky for me because the voices in my head that exhort me to self-harm are the same ones that have helped me to empathize with my neighbor.

In light of all this, my identity as a white male theologian living with depression is shaped by the tension I've described here. I am told that my condition—this depression—is a medical condition; that it is biological. It is in some sense as inescapable as my own skin, and it leads me to doubt whether my very being is something Jesus wants. And yet, in the despair born of such doubt, I encounter the truth of Scripture in new ways, and they in turn, nurture empathy and compassion with those who suffer most under our racist regime. Through my depression, I realize that my liberation is bound up with the liberation of the oppressed.

The paradox of my depression calls to mind the old children's hymn "I'll Be a Sunbeam," with lyrics by Nellie Talbot that state, "Jesus wants me for a sunbeam / To shine for him each day / In every way try to please him/ At home, at school, at play." That's a fine message for children perhaps, but the Scottish band the Vaselines have their own take on this song, one that begins, "Jesus don't want me for a sunbeam / 'Cause sunbeams are not made like me." That version rings true to me. I wasn't made to be a sunbeam, and this has made all the difference for me as a Christian and theologian.

14 An Unnatural Order

by RYAN DUECK

OVER THE LAST YEAR, I've been part of a community movement that has welcomed a number of Syrian refugee families to our small city on the Canadian prairies. Canada's refugee sponsorship model is unique in that groups of five or more individuals (often from churches or community groups) can privately sponsor refugees. This sponsorship entails looking after the refugees' financial needs for the first year and providing social support for the first year and beyond. Over the last ten months, I've found it richly rewarding to journey with our new Syrian friends.

But as delightful as it has been to watch my new friends take their first steps in our country, there are questions, too. How will this new reality change them and how they understand themselves? How will it change those of us who have been here for a long time? Although hands of friendship have been extended in both directions, their ways are somewhat strange to us, and ours are certainly strange to them. Things have to change when difference is introduced to any equation; we must adapt when we begin to bump up against people who have been shaped in contexts wildly different from our own.

This is a fascinating time to think about how we understand these questions, which all seem to hinge on some basic questions: Who am I? And who are we? These questions are not merely abstract ones for me or for the Syrian newcomers. So much of the news is driven by a resurgence of familiar identity markers in the face of threat—we look at Europe and observe the fear and tension that seems to dominate public consciousness. Whether it's the fallout of the migrant crisis that gripped our collective imaginations in the fall of 2015, with the photo of Syrian toddler Aylan Kurdi lying dead on a Turkish beach, or the perceived effects of longer-term patterns of immigration from troubled regions of the world, many people, both in Canada and south of the border, are wondering just how much difference can be absorbed while maintaining our existing identities and preserving peace.

Each week seems to produce a fresh new set of grim and foreboding headlines that jump out at us when we open our computers. Paris, Brussels, Istanbul, Baghdad, Nice, Manchester—it's not hard to imagine things getting worse. It's also not hard to imagine that the simmering resentment toward "outsiders" in Europe might erupt into much nastier and more overt forms of racism, religious intolerance, violence, and political instability. With the Brexit vote in our not-too-distant memory, it's not hard to imagine the European political landscape taking an abrupt turn toward the Right. Political parties representing the hard Right in Germany, Denmark, and the Netherlands are already making considerable gains in a sociopolitical context that is increasingly defined by polarization, extreme racial tension, and fear.

Many also fear what the Donald Trump presidency might add to the mix. Over the last year or so, we observed an American presidential race that was sharply divided along identity lines. We hear talk of walls being built to keep the wrong sorts of people out and to safeguard the privileges of the right sorts of people. We observe the scapegoating of Mexicans and Muslims, and we see deep racial tensions brought to the foreground when the spate of police shootings over the past year are answered by the triumphant call to "make America great again!" In light of the threats, tensions, and uncertainties our world is currently experiencing, many reflexively respond to Trump's call to return to familiar and self-protective lines and divisions between human beings.

These sociological, religious, and political realities are exerting pressure on how we form, maintain, and wrestle with questions of identity. They are creating new challenges and forming what may seem like impermeable boundaries between us and others. Given these challenges, I've been thinking more and more about whether there is a uniquely Christian contribution to the conversation. How ought our views of personal, ethnic, or even religious identity be shaped by the teachings of the God-man, Jesus of Nazareth?

One possible response to these questions comes from an unexpected, if tangentially related source. Several months ago, I read an article on adoption by J. D. Flynn at *First Things*. The gist of the piece was that adoption, while admirable in many ways, was a "deviation" from the natural order and that we should be doing more to render adoption unnecessary. The article didn't sit well with me, but at the time I didn't bother to think deliberately about why this was. Then, more recently, I reread the article and zeroed in on the following paragraph:

> But even in the most beautiful circumstances, adoption always represents a disruption to the natural order. Catholic social teaching emphasizes both the natural rights of children to their parents, and the supernatural privilege of parents to share in the procreative love of God the Father. . . . Adoption, by which natural parental rights are severed, is a deviation from that pattern.[1]

As an adoptive father, I am keenly aware that adoptive families face important challenges that "natural" families do not encounter, and I agree that there is an element of "tragic sadness" to all adoption stories. I am even prepared to admit that adoption can easily be romanticized and used for selfish ends. However, I also think Flynn has missed something crucial about God, adoption, and what that "natural order" looks like in God's arrangement of things.

Contrary to Flynn's interpretation, my sense is that the natural order, as established by the God revealed most clearly in Jesus Christ, is better characterized as bringing impossibly different people together and calling them family. The story of Scripture—and the story of God—is about the creation of a profoundly "unnatural order" and a new identity, one where Gentiles eat with Jews, tax collectors and prostitutes mingle with religious know-it-alls, and gender biases are abolished. The new world order is one where the last become first and the first become last; sinners and saints embrace, realizing they are one and the same; and every tribe and tongue is brought together by the one God who made and loves them all.

This vision is what gives me hope when I read of the roiling tensions and the refugee crisis in Europe or when I anxiously watched the presidential election unfold in the United States. This is how I think about myself and the world when I look to political hotspots like Israel and Palestine or when I think of the families I know and love that have kids with different colored skin and ethnic backgrounds. This Christian vision of identity grounds my conviction that our new Syrian friends do indeed belong with us and we with them. On a purely pragmatic level, it makes no sense to throw all this difference together in families and churches and cities and nations and to then expect it to end well. From that perspective, we should expect conflict and identity crises and scarcity and pain. We should bemoan disruptions in the natural order; we should cling to what is safe, predictable, and natural; we should tell people to stay where they belong.

But as followers of Jesus, we have been liberated from looking at things pragmatically. As followers of Jesus, we are free to imagine families, churches, cities, and

---

1. Flynn, "Adoption, Abortion, and a Message of Hope," *First Things*, August 27, 2015, https://www.firstthings.com/web-exclusives/2015/08/adoption-abortion-and-a-message-of-hope.

nations that struggle and strain and stretch toward the glorious reality of God's unnatural order. As followers of Jesus, we have been set free to ground our identities not in ethnicity or socioeconomic status or religion but in our shared humanity as dearly loved children of our stranger-welcoming and enemy-loving God.

Our present cultural moment asks a great deal of those of us who name Jesus as our Lord and teacher. It asks us to resist easy scapegoating and convenient boundary-maintenance. It asks us to not only decide to walk with open hands and generous hearts toward our neighbor but also to identify with them. This is a primary movement of faith. It is a way in which we imitate the way Christ moved toward us, calling us away from tribalistic allegiances to those with the right colored skin or the right flag or the right religion and toward the most unlikely of neighbors in love.

Faith ultimately asks us to remember and imagine differently as we think about who we are and how we belong in the world. In the Hebrew Bible, the divine command to care for the stranger is tied directly to the fact that the people of Israel were also once strangers in Egypt (e.g., Deut. 10:19). In the Gospel of Matthew, Jesus sums up all of the Law and the Prophets—and *all* is a surprisingly comprehensive word there—in the simple exhortation to do to others as we would have done to us (Matt. 7:12). The former urges us to better memory, the latter to better imagination. As followers of Jesus, we need both, if we are ever to learn who we really are, who we really should be, in and for the world.

15 Kinopolitics and the Figure of the Migrant: An Interview with Thomas Nail

by ZACHARY THOMAS SETTLE

IN HIS RECENT BOOK, *The Figure of the Migrant*, philosopher Thomas Nail highlights the migrant—the figure expelled from his or her home country—as the political figure of our time. In his insistence that these figures should reframe our entire understanding of political theory, Nail's work is both pressing and revelatory. In this interview, he discusses his recent work, speaking about the role of the migrant in the contemporary political landscape, the implications of that figure on our methods of theorization, and the ways in which migrants are constructively disruptive within our North American context.

The Other Journal (TOJ): In your recent book, *The Figure of the Migrant*, you argue that the figure of the migrant is the political figure of our time. You go on to analyze and question the foundational principles of the contemporary moment that gives rise to the migrant, and you speak of the migrant as a broader category of migratory figures, each of which are expelled from the dominant social order. This expulsion grounds, you argue, the figure of the migrant as the true motive force of social history.[1] Will you elaborate for us on your use of the term *figure of the migrant*? What characterizes such a figure, and what are the different ways in which you see that figure being employed in the global situation?

---

1. Nail, *The Figure of the Migrant* (Stanford, CA: Stanford University Press, 2015), 1 and 7.

Thomas Nail (TN): The migrant is the political figure who is socially expelled or dispossessed, to some degree as a result, or as the cause, of their mobility. We are not all migrants, but we are becoming migrants. At the turn of the twenty-first century, there were more regional and international migrants than ever before in recorded history. Today, there are over one billion migrants, and each decade the global percentage of migrants and refugees grows. Political theory has yet to take this phenomenon seriously. In *The Figure of the Migrant*, I argue that doing so requires political theory to alter its foundational presuppositions.

In my writing, I also consider four particular figures of the migrant: the nomad is the migrant who has been expelled from the territory; the barbarian is the migrant who has been expelled from political status or citizenship; the vagabond is the migrant who has been expelled from the juridical order; and the proletariat is the migrant who has been expelled from having control over the economic process. Each has its moment of historical emergence, each continues to coexist in the present, and each gives us a helpful framework for understanding contemporary migration.²

TOJ: In the introduction to your book, you argue that developing a political theory of the migrant that refuses to consider the figure as a failed citizen requires analyzing the figure according to its own defining feature: movement. This notion grounds your broader methodology and framework of kinopolitics, as you define the history of the migrant as one of social motion.³ Will you elaborate for us on your understanding and employment of this notion of movement and how that relates to your broader investigation of kinopolitics?

TN: Kinopolitics is the politics of movement, from the Greek word *kino*, meaning movement. If we are going to take the figure of the migrant seriously as a constitutive, and not derivative, figure of Western politics, we have to change the starting point of political theory. Instead of starting with a set of preexisting citizens, kinopolitics begins with the flows of migrants and the ways they have circulated or sedimented into citizens and states—as well as emphasizing how migrants have constituted a counterpower and alternative to state structures. In short, kinopolitics is the reinvention of political theory from the primacy of social motion instead of the state.

---

2. See Nail, *The Figure of the Migrant*; and Nail, "Migrant Cosmopolitanism," *Public Affairs Quarterly* 29, no. 2 (2015): 187–99, https://www.academia.edu/11784019/Migrant_Cosmopolitanism; Nail, "The Barbarism of the Migrant: Mexican Immigrants to the United States Face a Stigma that Stretches Back to Ancient Civilization," *Stanford University Press Blog*, September 2015, adapted from *The Figure of the Migrant*, http://stanfordpress.typepad.com/blog/2015/09/the-barbarism-of-the-migrant.html; and Nail, "The Hordes Are Banging on the Gates of Europe?" *History News Network*, October 25, 2015, https://www.academia.edu/17427414/The_Hordes_Are_Banging_on_the_Gates_of_Europe.

3. Nail, *The Figure of the Migrant*, 3 and 21.

It is because of the way that migrants move or don't move that they pose such difficulty for political theory and sedentary societies. In my book, I took this so-called exceptional attribute of motion and flipped the existing frameworks on their heads, interpreting motion as the primary feature of social life. Instead of looking at fixed subjects and objects, the book looks at "flows and junctions"; instead of looking at states and institutions, the book looks at "regimes of circulation." As it turns out, societies themselves are not, as they are often treated, static entities of fixed members but continuous circulations of metastable social flows. So I started with the migrant and ended up needing to build a new political theory to fit it. I think this method has produced some interesting and original conclusions.

TOJ: In the second part of *The Figure of the Migrant*, after sketching out your theory of the migrant, you employ a radicalization of Karl Marx's notion of primitive accumulation, originally found in Adam Smith's *Wealth of Nations*.[4] This notion, which you describe as "expansion by expulsion," serves to highlight the conditions through which the migrant is produced. You write that social expansion, as an exclusionary movement grounded in depriving one of social status, "is not simply the deprivation of territorial status (i.e., removal from the land); it includes three other major types of social deprivation: political, juridical, and economic."[5] Will you expand on that notion a bit, reflecting on your understanding of expansion by expulsion as it includes these different forms of social deprivation?

TN: The kinetic theory of expansion by expulsion is this: all hitherto existing societies have been able to expand—territorially, politically, juridically, economically—only on the condition of some kind and degree of prior social expulsion. The migrant is the figure of this expulsion. Marx was the first to identify this phenomenon with respect to the transition from feudalism to capitalism, but my thesis is not limited to this instance alone. Every major social formation has done something kinetically similar. The process of dispossessing migrants of their social status (i.e., expulsion) in order to further develop or advance a given form of social motion (i.e., expansion) is not unique to the capitalist regime of social motion.

We see this process of expansion by expulsion at work in early Neolithic societies whose progressive cultivation of land and animals (i.e., territorial expansion) would not have been possible without the expulsion (or territorial dispossession) of a part of the human population: hunter-gatherers, whose territory was transformed into agricultural land and who were themselves transformed into surplus agriculturalists for whom there was no more arable land left to cultivate at a certain point. Thus, social expulsion is the condition of social expansion in two ways: an internal condition

4. Ibid., 24.
5. Ibid., 35.

that allows for the removal of part of the population when certain internal limits have been reached (the carrying capacity of a given territory, for example) and an external condition that allows for the removal of part of the population outside these limits when the territory is able to expand outward into the lands of other groups (e.g., the hunter-gatherers). In this case territorial expansion was possible only on the condition that part of the population be expelled in the form of migratory nomads who were forced into the surrounding mountains and deserts.

Later, we see the same logic in the ancient world, whose dominant political form (i.e., the state) would not have been possible without the expulsion (i.e., political dispossession) of a large body of barbarian slaves kidnapped from the mountains of the Middle East and Mediterranean and used as workers, soldiers, and servants so that a growing ruling class could live in luxury. The social conditions for the expansion of a growing political order (including warfare, colonialism, and massive public works) were precisely the expulsion of a population of barbarians who had to be depoliticized at the same time. This occurs again and again throughout history. Each time, the regime of motion changes as does the figure of the migrant.

TOJ: I'm really intrigued by your understanding of the center—for example, the territory, state, or law—and its complicity in maintaining conditions by which the figure of the migrant is not only made possible but is also determined as the new norm. You point to Guy Geltner's work on the topic, in which he argues that the expansion of the juridical sphere required the management and capture of vagabonds in the early formation of the modern state.[6] Will you reflect for a bit on the ways in which the development of contemporary structures of law, state, border/territory, or free-market were developed in conjunction with the maintenance of migrants?

TN: This is a fascinating history that reveals the circular dictum of all juridical regimes: more laws produce more crime, and more crime requires more laws. Starting around the thirteenth century, peasants across continental Europe and Britain were expelled from their land through the abolition of customary laws, land tenure, and the introduction of land rent. Later, in sixteenth-century Britain, the privatization of peasant land for sheep grazing displaced tens of thousands of people. Throughout the West, the problem of migratory vagabonds or so-called "masterless men" was an enormous security threat. In order to deal with it, all kinds of new laws, officers, institutions, and so on were "needed" to lock people up, force them to work, transport them back and forth, and so on. An entire administrative apparatus began to emerge at this time that we call the early modern state. There is a long and interesting story here, but the conclusion is that the origins of the early modern state are tied directly to the expulsion of migrant vagabonds from their land. Without this expulsion, the

---

6. Geltner, *The Medieval Prison: A Social History* (Princeton, NJ: Princeton University Press, 2008).

prison apparatus and its proto-state correlates would have been entirely superfluous to the level of criminal mobility.

Something similar is still happening today in the West. The stricter the immigration laws, the more migrants are in violation of them; thus, criminal statistics reveal the "need" for harsher laws because of the "increase" in immigration violations. Migrants are a constitutive part of a juridical feedback mechanism that requires for its expansion the legal expulsion of a migrant population. I am not saying this is the conscious plot of some evil politicians—well, maybe Trump, but I hesitate to call him a politician—it's structural. It is part of the fundamental kinetic structure of juridical power.

TOJ: In your analysis of certain forms of migrancy, you argue that within pedetic motion—the motion of the foot defined by autonomy and self-motivation—lies the possibility for new forms of kinetic power that pose alternatives to social expulsion.[7] Your analysis revolves around the movement of the nomad, the barbarian, the vagabond, and the proletariat. What are the possibilities for social transformation made available in these alternative forms of movement, and how are they modeled in these varying forms of migrancy?

TN: In my work, I try both to do an analysis of the dominant forms of power in the West but also to study the forms of counter-power that emerge alongside them. The latter is decisively more difficult because history is so often written by the victors. The history of slave societies, maroon societies, communes, worker organizations, and other counter-powers has been systematically destroyed and rewritten, which makes it all the more important to gather and reinterpret what remains and to preserve what is currently being produced. So many times in my research I hit dead ends because of a lack of any primary documents or even secondary work on the topic of migrant counter-power—especially older forms of slave revolts and maroon societies that the Greeks and Romans systematically wrote out of history. Studying counter-power is hard. With the dominant forms of power, the problem is too much material to cover; with counter-power it's the opposite. And one reason we lack a good philosophical response to this problem is that philosophers tend to privilege written texts and achievements over material histories—and therefore, we unwittingly accept the bias of the victors. Philosophers write critiques of the dominant systems, but we lack a robust history of resistance.

In the book, I have tried to highlight these counter-powers, tracing some of the kinetic connections between non-state societies and the kind of dominant social motions that characterize them. These motions are, roughly, continuous oscillations,

---

7. Nail, *The Figure of the Migrant*, 125.

waves, and pressure. They are kinetic phenomena that are defined primarily by their pedetic motions. In social history, each figure of the migrant uses all three motions but also invents its own dominant counter-power tactic. Briefly, the nomad is associated with the development of the raid; the barbarian, the revolt; the vagabond, the rebellion; and the proletariat, resistance. Each type of tactic says something about the dominant type of kinopower it confronts and about the types of empirical alternatives created.

TOJ: In the fourth part of your book, you sketch out a theory of contemporary migration. You begin by explaining that migration has become increasingly complex and nuanced in the twentieth century and that the factors motivating these varied forms of movement range from economic deregulation and neoliberal development to technological transportation and communication. You argue that these social changes have given rise to a new form of hybridity in global migration, such that no singular theory will be sufficient in itself.[8] By redeploying the historical forms of social expansion by expulsion articulated earlier in the book (i.e., centripetal, centrifugal, tensional, and elastic forces), you diagnose historical, alternative forms of kinopolitical counter-power in contemporary migration. Will you discuss this theory of contemporary migration a bit for us?

TN: That was a pretty good summary. The process of expansion by expulsion and the figures of the migrant today are not new. They are a mixture of the processes and figures that have emerged historically and now mix together in new combinations. One consequence of this is that the study of migration in political theory needs to have a better grasp of the historical formations that constitute it. The empirical points may change, but the relations or forms of social motion repeat.

Most scholars write about migration as if it were a new area of study. Even when they talk about global migration, their studies usually only go back to the nineteenth century and they tend to focus on 1970s ideas of globalization, as if migration had never been global before that. This again may have to do with an overprivileging of written materials, texts, and statistics. Before the nineteenth century, there were far fewer statistics about migration; there were fewer books about migration; and there was almost no "scholarship" about migration. It is much easier to do scholarship that relies on other scholars in your area than to put together a synthetic history based on archeological, anthropological, and historical documents prior to the scholarly standardization of texts that emerges in the nineteenth century, and therefore, there is a real amnesia in the academy on the role of migrants in shaping our current and historical sociopolitical culture.

8. Ibid., 179.

16 handiwork

by OLUWATOMISIN OREDEIN

the juncture of beauty and cognition,
practicality and imagination—
these are our clothes.

we are wearing art.
unaware that we are muses,
we swim in conception,
sleep among wonder,
adjacent to inventiveness.

we are wearing art.
oblivious to our bodied significance,
stunning precisely
because we are canvas,
clay
and stone,
sand
and volcano.

our bodies—
surfaced wearings—
steer life into the center,
into stitches,
concentrated colors,
chaotic collaborations.

feverish
we glimpse the world
that will be

our skin

lovely
infinite.

Mark Wyatt, *Istanbul, Turkey*, 1980, photograph, Kodak Tri-X film. Courtesy of the artist.

17 Street Portraits: Anonymity as Identity

Photographs by MARK WYATT
Curated by JULIE M. HAMILTON

IN THESE IMAGES, WE find a collection of unrelated black-and-white portraits, taken on several different continents over the course of nearly forty years. Yet the artist, Mark Wyatt, is less interested in posing questions of context than inviting us to consider our relationship to the strangers we see depicted here. This kind of engagement with the photographic object performs a reciprocity of sight between the viewer and the viewed. States Wyatt: "The viewer's imagination is called forward to conjure up responses, and from those responses the viewer finds insight into his or her own identity." This perspective is indebted to the writings of philosopher Maurice Merleau-Ponty, whose phenomenology of perception configures vision as participation in the visible: "He who cannot possess the visible, unless he is possessed by it, unless he is of it, unless, by principle according to what is required by the articulation of the look with the things, he is one of the visibles, capable, by a singular reversal, of seeing them—he who is one of them."[1] Thus, Wyatt asks us to engage the universality of his subject's faces—looking beyond the location or year to the timelessness of human expression. He invites us to gaze at the stranger with vulnerability and empathy and, in turn, to allow our faces to mirror theirs. Through diversity and multiplicity, Wyatt hopes that we discover that what is shared in common—what Merleau-Ponty calls "the flesh of the world"—is indeed our own.

1. Merleau-Ponty, *The Visible and Invisible*, ed. Claude Lefort, trans. Alphonso Lingis, Studies in Phenomenology and Existential Philosophy (Evanston, IL: Northwestern University Press, 1968), 177–78.

Mark Wyatt, *Istanbul, Turkey*, 1980, photograph,
Kodak Tri-X film. Courtesy of the artist.

Mark Wyatt, *People's Republic of China*, 1995, photograph,
Fujicolor 200 film. Courtesy of the artist.

Mark Wyatt, *Barcelona, Spain*, 1980, photograph,
Kodak Tri-X film. Courtesy of the artist.

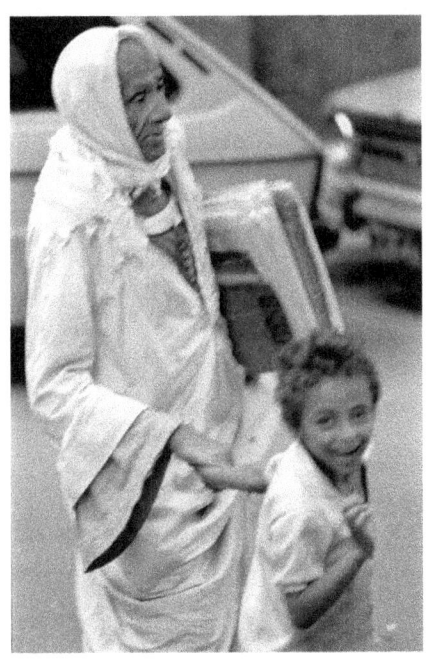

Mark Wyatt, *Cairo, Egypt*, 1980, photograph, Kodak Tri-X film. Courtesy of the artist.

Mark Wyatt, *Paris, France*, 1980, photograph, Kodak Tri-X film. Courtesy of the artist.

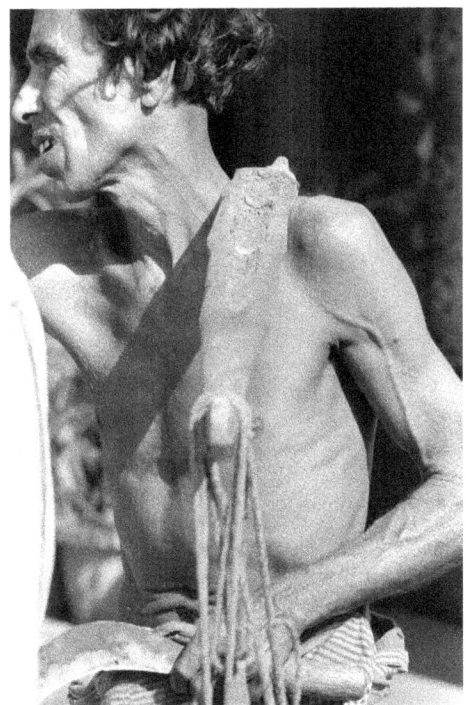

Mark Wyatt, *Calcutta, India*, 1980, photograph, Kodak Tri-X film. Courtesy of the artist.

Mark Wyatt, *Bayuquan, Peoples Republic of China*, 1995, photograph, Fujicolor 200 film. Courtesy of the artist.

Mark Wyatt, *Biarritz, France*, 1979, photograph, Kodak Tri-X film. Courtesy of the artist.

Mark Wyatt, *Trondheim, Norway*, 1980, photograph, Kodak Tri-X film. Courtesy of the artist.

Mark Wyatt, *Calcutta, India*, 1980, photograph, Kodak Tri-X film. Courtesy of the artist.

Mark Wyatt, *Hondarribia, Spain*, 2016, photograph, digital. Courtesy of the artist.

Mark Wyatt, *Tianjin, People's Republic of China*, 1995, photograph, Fujicolor 200 film. Courtesy of the artist.

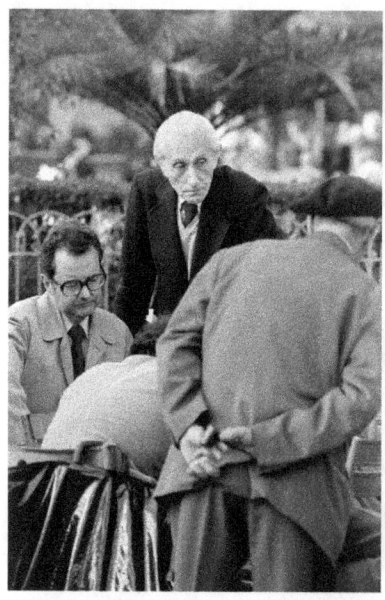 

Mark Wyatt, *Paris, France*, 1980, photograph, Kodak Tri-X film. Courtesy of the artist.

Mark Wyatt, *People's Republic of China*, 1995, photograph, Fujicolor 200 film. Courtesy of the artist.

Mark Wyatt, *Vienna, Austria*, 1980, photograph, Kodak Tri-X film. Courtesy of the artist.

18 Occupied Identity: The Aesthetics of Palestinian Suicide Bombing

by DEREK BROWN

THE ISRAELI OCCUPATION OF Palestine is ugly. To speak of the occupation as "ugly" may sound strange, jarring, or at least atypical. But I suggest that, at its core, occupation is an aesthetic phenomenon and one that we must investigate theologically.[1] There is no beauty in occupation, but this does not mean that we cannot conduct an aesthetic analysis, that we cannot consider how matter and relationships are aesthetically manipulated. The opposite is the case. Precisely because there is no beauty in occupation, precisely because occupation is so ugly, we must take on the project of aesthetic critique. Aesthetically, occupation takes the form of walls, borders, and checkpoints. It is the despair that infects relationships. And it is the objectified flesh of suicide bombers.[2]

---

1. There are other points of departure for addressing this question. A profanely historical survey of the occupation might be useful insofar as an archaeology of occupation could be used to destabilize current norms. But historical surveys have been done, especially by Ilan Pappé. Scanning the academic and popular literature suggests other, perhaps more nuanced, approaches. Postcolonial theory is crucial in Palestinian studies, but here I have little to add to the work of Edward Said. Theologically, one can take the standpoint of the Palestinian liberation theology developed by Naim Ateek.

2. Classically, aesthetics is the philosophy of perception. That theological aesthetics could partake in and further this tradition by taking as its object the *perception of creation*—of created matter—seems, to me, unobjectionable. That theological aesthetics should also deal with liberation has been convincingly argued by Roberto Goizueta in his *Christ Our Companion: Toward a Theological Aesthetics of Liberation* (Maryknoll, NY: Orbis, 2009).

SUICIDE BOMBING

Palestinian suicide bombings were most prevalent during the period known as the Second Intifada. Precise dates are disputed and perhaps unimportant, but the Second Intifada lasted roughly from September 2000, when former Israeli Minister of Foreign Affairs Ariel Sharon made a provocative and aggressive visit to Temple Mount in Old City Jerusalem, to February 2005, when Palestinian President Mahmoud Abbas and then Prime Minister Sharon agreed to the Sharm el-Sheikh Summit agreement, which promised an end to Israeli military activity against Palestinians. Between 2000 and 2005, there were 241 suicide attacks done by Palestinians. By way of comparison, between 1980 and 2005, there were twenty-three attacks. Since 2005, there have been seven. Since 2008, there has been only one: in 2015, a Palestinian woman exploded a bomb in her car after she was stopped by Israeli traffic police on her way to Jerusalem. She was the only fatality.[3]

Despite the fact that suicide bombing is no longer the predominant tool of resistance—which is always the same as saying that it is no longer the predominant means of occupation—the sheer and deep ugliness of this particular act demonstrates, in a marked and moving way, the terror of the Israeli occupation of Palestine.[4] The ugliness of the act compels us to look. But if we glance too quickly, we might see the suicide bombings as a chance to apologize for occupation: *these people kill the innocent; they must be occupied.* So, true to the spirit of immanent criticism, we will overcome this apologetic claim by going through it. If suicide bombing is held as the grounds of occupation, then these grounds should be shaken.

To date, the most thorough and convincing theological discussion of Palestinian suicide bombing is Naim Ateek's 2002 essay "Suicide Bombers: What Is Theologically and Morally Wrong with Suicide Bombing?" The essay is a careful and nuanced "attempt to understand but not justify" suicide bombing.[5] Ateek argues that

---

3. See "Terrorism, Counterterrorism, and Unconventional Warfare," Johnston's Archive, February 22, 2016, http://www.johnstonsarchive.net/terrorism/; "Terrorism against Israel: Comprehensive Listing of Fatalities (September 1993–present)," Jewish Virtual Library, http://www.jewishvirtuallibrary.org/jsource/Terrorism/victims.html; and "Suicide and Other Bombing Attacks in Israel since the Declaration of Principles (Sept 1993), Israel Ministry of Foreign Affairs, http://www.mfa.gov.il/mfa/foreignpolicy/terrorism/palestinian/pages/suicide%20and%20other%20bombing%20attacks%20in%20israel%20since.aspx.

4. Lately, heartbreakingly, there has been an increase—not a decrease—in suicide bombings outside of Israel/Palestine. These suicide bombings, which have attacked both the West—France and Belgium—and the Middle East—Turkey and Beirut—demand a different aesthetic analysis. The relationship here between occupied and occupier is not, to me, clear at all. I suspect it is not clear to the bombers, either. The fact that these attacks are done alongside of shootings and other means of murder also demands a different aesthetics—this will become more clear as my analysis of the fleshly nature of suicide bombings plays out. Regardless, I am concerned here with Palestine. But these recent events are on my mind and cannot be totally compartmentalized, so they are thus present.

5. Ateek, "Suicide Bombers: What is Theologically and Morally Wrong with Suicide Bombing? A

suicide bombing is, incontrovertibly, a response to occupation. With characteristic directness, he captures the gravity of this situation:

> When healthy, beautiful, and intelligent young men and women set out to kill and be killed, something is basically wrong in a world that has not heard their anguished cry for justice. These young people deserve to live along with all those whom they have caused to die.[6]

Continuing along moral lines, now laced with a more overtly theological bent, Ateek notes that suicide bombings are done from a place of total despair. This category of despair, for Ateek, is essential for any understanding of suicide bombing.[7] The story of one suicide bomber, Abdel Odeh, is taken as demonstrative:

> Odeh was prevented by the Israeli authorities from crossing into Jordan to get married to his fiancée from Baghdad. The Israeli Shin Bet (security intelligence) kept sending after him. He refused to go because he suspected, as often happens, that they would blackmail and pressure him into becoming an informer. He was twenty-five years old, ready to get married, start a family, settle in Jordan, and enjoy life. When everything was shut in his face and his future plans were shattered by the Israeli army, he turned to suicide bombing. His father attributed his son's action to humiliation and a broken heart. His family first heard about the bombing from the television. Such stories abound in the Palestinian community.[8]

Odeh's story and others like it show the ways in which Palestinian subjectivity is constructed to be despairing. The occupation creates an environment where despair is the norm—the occupied do not despair *for* something, but they are constructed as despairing, as dehumanized.

A despairing life, especially one under occupation, makes one capable of things unimaginable to those of us who live more comfortably. This is not to say that the conditions in Palestine are so horrid that suicide is the only option. No, far from it. Rather, the occupation is so brutal and it employs aesthetics in such a perverse way that suicide bombing becomes an imaginable act. Occupation sets the conditions for its own violent resistance. As Ateek has demonstrated, this violence is the result of despair, which is itself the result of the *material* and *relational*—that is, the

---

Palestinian Christian Perspective," *Studies in World Christianity* 8, no. 1 (2008): 5–30, 7.

6. Ibid., 5.

7. Ibid., 8. Ateek is firm that suicide bombing is the result of despair: "There were no suicide bombings before the Oslo Peace Process. It is the result of despair and hopelessness that started to set in when an increasing number of Palestinians became frustrated by the deepening Israeli oppression and humiliation." Again: "And as (Palestinians) were driven deeper into despair, their desire to hit back in any way possible grew in intensity."

8. Ibid., 8.

aesthetic—instantiations of occupation. These material instantiations of occupation, such as checkpoints and Israeli-operated prisons, affect Palestinian relationality in destructive ways: they make the family unstable, alienate the worker, and establish a hierarchy in which the most stable relationships are between the occupied and the occupier. Put differently, occupation makes matter and relationships *ugly* things. Aesthetics is used as a tool of occupation, so a theological response to occupation must have at its disposal tools capable of critiquing constructions of beauty and ugliness.

CRITICAL THEOLOGICAL AESTHETICS

By speaking of beauty and ugliness, I am not primarily interested in what beauty *is*. Rather, I am interested in what beauty—as construct, category, signifier—*does*.[9] Concern for what beauty does is what makes a theological aesthetics properly critical because it critiques particular deployments and constructions of beauty, and it does so with an eye toward liberation and justice. And it is in this respect that Theodor Adorno's critical aesthetics offers a compelling and theologically provocative way forward. For Adorno, the fundamental aesthetic act is renunciation. Beauty is that which renounces the ugly.

Adorno notes that the ugly is intimately bound up with suffering: "The aesthetic condemnation of the ugly is dependent on the inclination, verified by social psychology, to equate, justly, the ugly with the expression of suffering and, by projecting it, to despise it."[10] Ugliness as suffering seems to make good phenomenological sense, but phenomenology is not what Adorno is doing. By identifying ugliness with suffering he is not making a claim as to some essence of ugliness. Rather, Adorno is arguing that the category of ugliness is employed in such a way as to aesthetically value suffering. What counts as suffering is mediated aesthetically. That is, suffering is deemed ugly when one wants to be rid of it. At the same time, the oppressed, those who suffer under oppression, are deemed ugly by virtue of the fact that they have been renounced by their oppressors.

We must recognize that Adorno is here simpatico with Ateek: "If Israel labels (suicide bombers) as terrorists, they are, after all, the product of its own making."[11] Nobody is born a suicide bomber. Instead, barriers, checkpoints, and squalid conditions

---

9. With this, I intend to join the ranks of theologians like M. Shawn Copeland, Maureen H. O'Connell, and Roberto Goizueta, all of whom are involved in a critical theological aesthetics. Whether or not Hans Urs von Balthasar's project is "critical" in this sense is a topic large and complex enough for a book. There are assuredly both tensions and resonances between von Balthasar's aesthetics and liberation theology.

10. Adorno, *Aesthetic Theory*, trans. Robert Hullot-Kentor (Minneapolis, MN: University of Minnesota Press, 1996), 49.

11. Ateek, "Suicide Bombers," 8.

all yell out, as it were, *You, you are a terrorist!* Occupation occupies Palestinian matter and relationships—it renounces them and thus makes them ugly.

MATERIALITY

There is an inherent relationship between aesthetics and politics. Or rather, there is an aesthetic mediation of the political. Relationships of power—those relationships between the oppressed and the oppressor—give themselves in aesthetic forms. It is not just that politics constructs notions of the beautiful; in such a schema, aesthetics would be reducible to the political. Rather, aesthetics is political because it names suffering as ugly, and so as undesirable. But this undesirability can be read in different ways. For the oppressor, the goal is clear: We are to treat the ugly as really ugly. We are to ignore them, accept their dehumanized form, and perhaps even blame their ugliness for causing this neglect—*if you weren't so vile, I would offer to help.* But from the standpoint of the Christian tradition, the ultimate aesthetic act is God's becoming flesh. In taking up flesh, God takes up a space and a body in our shared aesthetic history. God becomes a human person who can be perceived and who can perceive with us. Because God became incarnate—and so made and affirmed the beauty of humanity—we must renounce all oppressive attempts of naming people, *especially suffering people*, as ugly. In this way, the fundamental theological aesthetic act is the renunciation of oppression.

God's aesthetic call, the call of beauty, is never merely to admire God's beauty, but it is also to perceive and do beauty as Christ did. As the "light of the human race" (John 1:4 NABRE), Christ illumines not only divine truth but also flesh itself. In this way, the incarnation is a radical materialization of beauty. Beauty cannot be merely transcendent because absolute beauty, Christ himself, was made of matter; Christ ate with us, walked with us, and gazed with us. By doing miracles here in the flesh—miracles that were, by the way, concerned with physical well-being, with feeding and healing—Jesus brought beauty here, to the flesh. Hence, Christ unsettles the old and worn distinction between "divine" and "worldly" or "supernatural" and "natural" beauty. Theologically, we can speak plainly of beauty and ugliness. The incarnation encourages us to speak of participating and renouncing, in the flesh, in the material world, with Christ. Thus, the kingdom of heaven, understood as the way and life revealed by Christ's life that is both already here and not-yet-here, is not only a spiritual one. In order to truly partake in the building of the kingdom, we must constantly negate instances of ugly materiality.

The institution of the checkpoint, which is just one instance of occupation, does not partake in the building of such a kingdom. It partakes in creating a materially ugly world: there are no checkpoints in heaven; divinized flesh ought not be subjected to checkpoints. The ugliness of checkpoints refers not so much to the architecture of the checkpoints—although they are daunting and dim—but to the fact that checkpoints and barriers, contribute to the notion that matter itself is oppressive. The depth of the ugliness of a checkpoint can best be seen when contrasted with a home, a place of protection and love. G. W. F. Hegel's famous meditation on home construction shows this ugliness. The home, Hegel teaches, is built using the laws of nature and the stuff of nature in order to restrain nature:

> So also when someone starts building a house, his decision to do so is freely made. But all the elements must help. And yet the house is being built to protect man against the elements. Hence the elements are here used against themselves. But the general law of nature is not disturbed thereby. . . . The result is that the wind, which has helped to build the house, is shut out by the house; so also are the violence of rains and floods and the destructive powers of fire, so far as the house is made fire-proof. The stones and beams obey the law of gravity and press downwards so that the high walls are held up. Thus the elements are made use of in accordance with their nature and cooperate for a product by which they become constrained.[12]

And so a home is an exercise in cooperation between a builder and nature. Nature is cooperative, and matter is protective. To some extent, matter is even sacrificial: matter undermines itself, keeps itself out, in order to protect the builder and the home-dweller.

But this is not the relationship between matter and a checkpoint. In a checkpoint, matter is used not to protect but to keep out. The checkpoint forces the Palestinian to submit to the will of the Israeli. Here, at the checkpoint, the aesthetics are that of the butcher's corral: dehumanized bodies are pushed this way, flopped that way, stripped over here, tossed over there. The checkpoint, as Ateek notes, is "clearly a policy that strips people of their self worth and dignity."[13] But the checkpoint is not just a policy; it is also a place and a site built of matter. And, as Ateek also notes, it is a site that is often "arbitrarily mounted at whim." In this way, the checkpoint is a site of construction—quite literally, with gates and walls and fences and blocks and turrets—that dehumanizes human beings. Matter, allied with occupation, is dehumanizing. Matter turns a complex human into simple matter. It is thus no mystery that the suicide bomber thinks of himself as a *that* instead of a *who*. Those on the ugly side of the checkpoint see the matter of nature used to aid in their oppression and occupation. Their occupation depends on material stuff. Matter is oppressive.

---

12. Hegel, "A General Introduction to the Philosophy," in *Reason in History*, trans. Robert S. Hartman (Upper Saddle River, NJ: Prentice Hall, 1953), 34.

13. Ateek, "Suicide Bombers," 9.

A critical theological aesthetics renounces this perspective, and the dehumanizing structures that foster this perspective, by way of a double liberation. First, matter itself is liberated. Matter ought not be thought of as oppressive because God both created and became matter, and God is not oppressor. Second, those who suffer checkpoints must be liberated, and a constituent element of this liberation is the transfiguration of their world. If the matter that surrounds the occupied remains oppressive, then they can never be free.

The failure to liberate those who suffer checkpoints—for example, the Palestinians—has resulted in a terrible fulfillment of the logic of oppressive matter: the apparent oppressiveness of matter finds fulfillment in the reduction of the person to weapon, as suicide bombers use, abuse, and sacrifice their materiality in order to annihilate the materiality of themselves and others. Murder by gun uses matter to kill, but firearms and bullets are not people—they are not flesh. Murder by suicide, though, makes the place and matter that is a human person into a site of destructive resistance. The bomber is converted from person to weapon. The aesthetics of the bomber are irrevocably changed; the body becomes a weapon, changed from whom to that. The suicide bomber does not throw an explosive at the victims. Rather, the suicide bomber becomes the explosive.

And so suicide bombing is a hatred of self and other that treats flesh as inhuman matter. But the suicide bomber is not responsible for this reduction. As Ateek says, "It was in the crucible of the occupation that [suicide bombers] were shaped and formed."[14] This reduction of human flesh to a dangerous weapon is done by the occupier. It is the occupier who constructs Palestinian identity in such a way that bodies are always already weaponized. Suicide bombing, then, is a response to this occupation of the flesh. Palestinian flesh is made ugly by occupation and made a weapon, a terrorist, by the checkpoint.

RELATIONALITY

Ateek says that there is "hardly any Palestinian family in the West Bank and the Gaza Strip that has not experienced some kind of pain or injury."[15] The statistics agree: There are more than 4.5 million Palestinian refugees worldwide. The current population of the Palestinian territories is also, roughly, 4.5 million. A Palestinian today is just as likely to be a refugee as she is to live in Palestine. During the Second Intifada, it is estimated that 4,800 Palestinians were killed. Another 2,000 were killed during the First Intifada, which is known as the peaceful intifada. The 1982 Lebanon War, Israel's invasion of southern Lebanon, resulted in up to 20,000 Palestinian deaths. The

14. Ibid., 8.
15. Ibid., 9.

assaults are so common that Israel calls its intrusions into Gaza "mowing the lawn."[16] The frequency of violence has made violence the norm. Speaking to this heartbreaking reality, Noam Chomsky notes, "Israel killed, on average, more than two Palestinian children a week for the past 14 years."[17] On average, including times of "peace" and times of open slaughter, two children are killed a week. To live in Palestine is to live familiarly with death.

These statistics confirm what the fact of suicide bombing already suggests: there is despair. Such a constant threat of death necessarily changes one's understanding of relationship. A properly theological aesthetics claims that relationality is expansive and promising: Christ is the promise that brings us past the limit of ugliness, and relationship is the promise of hope.[18] In Palestine, though, relationships often bring the promise of more despair.

These relationships of despair are illustrated, literally, in Palestinian street art. Indeed, the aesthetic presence of death is ubiquitous in Gaza. Journalist Eóin Murray describes this presence:

> The street art here in Gaza focuses primarily on the human element of loss. On every street corner, in almost every shop (sometimes because they want to, sometimes because of social and political pressure) there are photographs and paintings of the dead, mostly young men but also women and children—people who have been killed by the Israeli army. . . . The street art celebrates the faces of martyrs and largely it is a simple form of painting, almost in pre-renaissance style with little attention paid to perspective or to any sense of a da Vinci-esque homage to human detail. . . . They usurp symbols such as the dove or flowers—showing them as they wither away under the occupation. The collective suffering of the people is emphasized by the huddled crowds which appear on this and other murals. Of course, this is in stark contrast to the immediate sense of the individual one absorbs from the murals of the "martyrs." These individuals faced their death alone and are celebrated alone, on large murals, or small posters, with a background of flowers and weaponry. Guns 'n' Roses.[19]

In paying homage to the martyr, the audience is forming a relationship to death-as-image. Thus, these murals do away with the aesthetic category of promise and, with it, hope. These murals are blunt, as if to say: *There is no beauty. Let's skip the happiness; let's get to the meat of the matter. This is the limit. This society is unhappy; there*

16. Noam Chomsky, "Ceasefires in which Violations Never Cease: What's Next for Israel, Hamas, and Gaza?," TomDispatch.com, September 9, 2014, http://www.tomdispatch.com/blog/175892/.

17. Ibid.

18. See Goizueta, *Christ Our Companion*.

19. Murray, "The Art of War," The Electronic Intifada, January 13, 2005, https://electronicintifada.net/content/art-war/5418.

is no way out. In occupation, the aesthetic object becomes an image not of beauty but of death itself. The status quo is death, and these murals represent that. And so the viewer's relationship to the aesthetic image is one of despair, of sameness, and of death.

And so for the Palestinian, relationships to aesthetic objects are not relationships to hopeful beauty but rather the opposite: they are relationships to death. Beauty offers the potential to renounce occupation, to name occupation ugly, but there is no relationship to beauty here. The most stable relationship the occupied has is with the occupier; given the apparent omnipotence of the occupier, this is the only relationship that promises to stay. Instead of participation and beautification, then, this is an aesthetics of sameness. Hope and beauty are themselves renounced. It is thus no mystery that the Palestinian suicide bomber offers death to the Israeli, for it is death that the Israeli offers to the Palestinian suicide bomber.

ON TO BEAUTIFYING

For Ateek, suicide bombing must be condemned because it disregards the value of life. But this disregard works from both ends: the Israeli disregards the Palestinian, and the Palestinian bomber disregards the Israeli. Therefore, we can say that suicide bombing must be condemned because it is both a construction and a promulgation of ugliness: the Israeli creates ugly matter and relationships, and the Palestinian bomber affirms the ugliness of these things through suicide bombing. There is no promise, no hope, and thus no beauty. We seem trapped. How can beauty promise change where ugliness begets itself?

Yet, Ateek, at least in 2002, in a time of increased violence, remains hopeful:

> All peace-loving people, whether people of faith or not, must exert greater concerted effort to work for the ending of the occupation. Ultimately, justice will prevail, the occupation will be over, and the Palestinians, as well as the Israelis, will enjoy freedom and independence. How do I know that this will take place? I know because I believe in God.[20]

Despite Chomsky's dire concern, and despite the horror and heartbreak of Israel's most recent episode of "mowing the lawn," there may be reason to share Ateek's hope.[21] If Ateek is right that suicide bombing is a result of despair, then the decreased

20. Ateek, "Suicide Bombers," 26–27.

21. Israel's 2014 "Operation Protective Edge," which is an English translation designed to convey defensiveness and innocence and is more literally translated as "Operation Strong Cliff," was a performance of war crimes widely renounced by international legal and faith communities. Succumbing to tears, Chris Gunness, chief spokesperson for the United Nations Relief and Works Agency for Palestine, summarized the operation: "What is happening in Gaza, particularly to the children, is an affront to the humanity of all of us." Gunness's work is important, laudable, and saintly. These particular words

frequency of suicide attacks may be a sign of hope among the Palestinians. If my analysis is right that suicide bombing is a reduction of Palestinian flesh to a weapon and an acceptance of the finitude of relationships, then the decreased frequency of attacks may be a sign of the return of the flesh and a righting of relationships—a sort of return of the repressed. The cause of this return can only be speculated—perhaps greater international solidarity, especially from the Boycott, Divestment and Sanctions movement, has reclaimed the category of relationship. Or perhaps the Israeli Left, which is offering a domestic challenge to Prime Minister Benjamin Netanyahu, has shown that occupation need not be infinite. More radically, perhaps occupation itself is instable, and ultimately the beauty of relationships and matter cannot be totally reduced. Indeed, Adorno seemed open to such a notion.[22]

Of course, Israelis disagree that there is any such return. Their explanation for the decrease in bombings is more practical: the Netanyahu regime and the Israel lobby have credited the construction of security fences with deterring bombers.[23] But this claim does not hold up to scrutiny: there has still been violence. Indeed, there has been talk of a third intifada, the "Knife Intifada" or "Lone Wolf Intifada." No, violence has not stopped; violence has changed. Would-be suicide bombers now kill with a knife instead of with their bodies. This is deplorable, but it is different. Without valorizing these knife attacks, we can say, "Thankfully, we no longer see suicide bombings in Palestine or Israel."

We hope that these bombings do not return. We also hope that their absence is a sign of diminishing despair, a sign of hope and beauty. Perhaps there are no longer suicide bombers because there are no longer Palestinians who have internalized the dehumanization dished out by the programs of Israeli occupation. That is, perhaps suicide bombing and the oppressive structures that have created it are being renounced.

To conclude, I turn to a text that has inspired the argument from the beginning, if only in unstated terms. The prologue to the Gospel of John shows that Christ's divine renunciation, the theological aesthetic moment par excellence, has unexpected contours. Eventually, we see, renunciation itself is beautified:

> In the beginning was the Word, and the Word was with God, and the Word was God. He was in the beginning with God. All things came to be through him, and without him nothing came to be. What came to be through him

---

are moving, prophetic, and beautiful; "UN Spokesperson Chris Gunness Breaks Down during Interview on Gaza," *Guardian* video, July 31, 2014, https://www.theguardian.com/world/video/2014/jul/31/un-spokesman-chris-gunness-breaks-down-during-aljazeera-interview-video.

22. See Adorno, "Culture Industry Reconsidered," in *The Culture Industry: Selected Essays on Mass Culture*, ed. J. M. Bernstein (London, UK: Routledge, 1999), 98–106.

23. Mitchell Bard, "West Bank Security Fence: Background and Overview," Jewish Virtual Library, February 2016, https://www.jewishvirtuallibrary.org/jsource/Peace/fence.html.

> was life, and this life was the light of the human race; the light shines in the darkness, and the darkness has not overcome it. . . . And the Word became flesh and made his dwelling among us, and we saw his glory, the glory as of the Father's only Son, full of grace and truth. (John 1:1–5, 14)

In order to do beauty, Christ subjects himself to the ugliness of the world. Christ did not come only as flesh, but as poor flesh, ugly flesh. He came as occupied Palestinian flesh. The ultimate beauty of Christ is found in his ability to see the darkness through to its end. Because Christ did not accept the darkness of his oppressors, we can now hope that "the light shines in the darkness, and the darkness has not overcome it." We need not be suicide bombers—but as I have argued, this is the same as saying, we need not accept occupation. The darkness of occupation is an ugliness that begets itself. In this sense, all occupation is anti-Christ. Our choice, then, is quite clear: renounce Christ by endorsing the occupation he came to overturn or renounce *with* Christ by renouncing the ugliness, by healing the suffering, and by beautifying the desecration that we have allowed.

19 Can't Stop the Feelings: Anger and Identity in Mark 6:17–29

by ANGELA PARKER

Identities are embodied horizons from which we each must confront and negotiate our shared world and specific life condition.
—LINDA MARTIN ALCOFF, *VISIBLE IDENTITIES*

WHILE TEACHING AN INTRODUCTORY class on the New Testament, I called on a student to read a portion of the Gospel of John. Before jumping into the text, the student noted that I seem to get angry when my students read from what I deem unapproved translations. I waited a moment and then said, "You all have never seen me angry. I am a black women from South Jersey. You'll know I am angry when I take off my earrings, because then I am ready to fight." My anecdote of course highlights a relationship between context, anger, and action, but more particularly, it hints at the way angry black women have engaged in specific actions in order to make changes in society.

One such instance is the case of Bree Newsome, who scaled a thirty-foot flagpole at the South Carolina State House and took down the Confederate flag, a symbol embraced by the gunman who murdered nine black parishioners during a Bible study ten days earlier in Charleston, South Carolina.[1] Reports stated that as

---

1. See Jesse James DeConto, "Activist Who Took Down Confederate Flag from Statehouse Drew on

Newsome ascended the pole, she shouted that "in the name of Jesus, this flag has to come down." Then, as she was arrested, onlookers could hear her reciting Psalm 23.

At that particular moment in history, a self-identified black female Christian demonstrated her religious values while negotiating her world and life condition in order to remove a cultural representation that demeaned her identity. Newsome's faith, in this sense, sought to challenge a system that often allows easy forgiveness to perpetuate racism.

Yet when black women perform acts of aggression as legitimate reactions to unequal circumstances, society often dubs them pathological, irrational, and angry.[2] This has led me to wonder how other women identified as "angry" black Christians in the age of #BlackLivesMatter are trying to transform a system that receives impunity when it murders black and brown bodies. Turning to the story of Herodias in the Gospel of Mark helps me ponder my own identity and so-called anger issues.

Contrary to traditional interpretations that blame Herodias for the death and beheading of John the Baptist, I imagine Herodias in her context. I picture her as a mother raising a daughter in the midst of Roman imperial politics and violence. Reframing Herodias in this way prompts the following questions: As a woman who is close to power but still lacks power since she *is* a woman, what was Herodias really trying to behead? How does the Markan characterization of Herodias's anger affect our interpretation? To that end, I argue that interpreters of the Herodias story must engage a nuanced reading of her identity and anger. By contextualizing the one-dimensional identity that the Markan writer places upon her, I see Herodias as a woman who seeks to behead male political authority over female bodies, lives, and inheritance. Just as Herodias works to navigate her world, so too must I as a black Christian woman continue to nuance my identity even as I am angry at the systematic injustice of our world.

IDENTITY AND WOMANIST ANGER

In the opening epigraph, I invoke Linda Martin Alcoff's definition of identity as "embodied horizons from which we each must confront and negotiate our shared world and specific life condition."[3] In placing identity within the idea of "embodied horizons," she helpfully brings its discussion into contact with the aims

---

Faith, Civil Rights Awakening," *Christian Century* 132, no. 17 (2015): 15–16.

2. For cogent discussions on the "angry black woman" myth and stereotype, see Melissa V. Harris-Perry, *Sister Citizen: Shame, Stereotypes, and Black Women in America* (New Haven, CT: Yale University Press, 2011); Lakesia D. Johnson, *Iconic: Decoding Images of the Revolutionary Black Woman* (Waco, TX: Baylor University Press, 2012); and Sophia A. Nelson, *Black Woman ReDefined, Dispelling Myths and Discovering Fulfillment in the Age of Michelle Obama* (Dallas, TX: BenBella Books, 2011).

3. Alcoff, *Visible Identities: Race, Gender, and the Self* (New York, NY: Oxford University Press, 2006), 288–89.

of contemporary hermeneutics, which is broadly concerned with the question of human understanding.[4] Alcoff uses Hans-Georg Gadamer's concept of the "fusion of horizons" in order to show the ways in which one can only know one's own identity through engaging with other people, texts, and works of art. Contact with an "other" forever changes a person as a result of that fusion. With regard to race and gender as visible identities, Alcoff argues against critiques of identity; she contends that identities provide us with narratives that explain the links between group historical memory and individual, contemporary experience. Identity creates unifying frames that render experiences intelligible, help people map their social world, and serve as tools for meaning-making.[5]

Alcoff refers to the identities imposed on people from the outside as a sort of "branding."[6] Within the cultural milieu of the United States, the branding of black women has been so pervasive that it permeates the lived experiences of black women in a tangible, violent way. Only after fully understanding the identity formation of black women can we confront the lived experiences that result from the branding that forms identity. Thus, an ethics informed by womanist scholarship, which privileges the lives and experiences of black women, is important for understanding the stereotypical identity that society has placed upon black women in general.[7]

One author who specifically speaks to womanist identity is Emilie Townes. In her work, Townes addresses the imposed identity of black women through an analysis of what she calls the "cultural production of evil" or the way in which white society systematically perpetuates the misery and suffering of black women by acting

---

4. For an excellent delineation of hermeneutics as an early theory and its subsequent evolution, see Stanley E. Porter and Jason C. Robinson, *Hermeneutics: An Introduction to Interpretative Theory* (Grand Rapids, MI: Eerdmans, 2011) 1–21.

5. Alcoff points out that political arguments behind the critique of identity can be boiled down to the following three: (1) strongly felt ethnic or cultural identities will inevitably produce a problem of conflicting loyalties within a larger grouping, such as a nation; (2) identities encourage the reification of group identities that lead to conformism, intolerance, and patriarchalism, thus curtailing individuals' ability to creatively interpret their identities; and (3) identities pose a problem for rational deliberation, especially over public ends. Rationality mandates that we must be able to subject the claims embedded in cultural traditions to rational reflection, and this requires achieving enough distance from our social identities that we can objectify and thus evaluate them. In essence, everyone must be mainstream (i.e., white). See Alcoff, *Visible Identities*, 36–38, 41.

6. Ibid., 42.

7. By focusing specifically on black women, womanism aims for the transformation of society and liberation of all people in the black community. Some seminal texts include Jacquelyn Grant, *White Women's Christ, Black Women's Jesus: Feminist Christology and Womanist Response* (Atlanta, GA: Scholars Press, 1989); Katie Cannon, *Black Womanist Ethics* (Atlanta, GA: Scholars Press, 1988); Cannon, *Katie's Canon: Womanism and the Soul of the Black Community* (New York, NY: Continuum, 1995); Cheryl Kirk-Duggan, *Exorcising Evil: Theodicy and African American Spirituals—A Womanist Perspective* (Maryknoll, NY: Orbis, 1993); Emilie Maureen Townes, *Womanist Justice, Womanist Hope* (Atlanta, GA: Scholars Press, 1993); and Townes, *A Troubling in My Soul: Womanist Perspectives on Evil and Suffering* (Maryknoll, NY: Orbis, 1993).

as if their identity to exist only occurs insofar as it is affirmed by the arbiters of the status quo. Referring to this implicit authoritarian perspective, Townes argues that white supremacy has constructed a "fantastic hegemonic imagination" wherein society identifies black women in five caricatures: Aunt Jemima, Sapphire, the Tragic Mulatta, the Welfare Queen, and Topsy.[8]

Placing Townes in conversation with Alcoff as I consider Mark 6:19–27 leads me to wonder whether Herodias has fallen prey to the fantastic hegemonic imagination within biblical scholarship. How should a womanist engage Herodias's female identity and anger? Or more particularly, how should I, as a self-identified black, Christian, female scholar, engage Herodias in a way that contextualizes my own anger and what I perceive as Herodias's anger within the biblical text?

THE STICKINESS OF READING AS AN "ANGRY" BLACK WOMAN

Traditionally, historical biblical scholarship has sought to find the *objective* reading of Scripture. Reader-response criticism, however, aims to take the identity of the reader more seriously. An author can write a text, but unless someone reads (or hears) the text, communication does not occur. Accordingly, meaning-making occurs between the text and the auditor/reader. Just as first-century auditors of Mark's gospel had to make decisions about how they heard and understood the text, as a contemporary black Christian woman, I must make key decisions on how I read and understand the text.

Contrary to historical biblical scholarship, reader-response criticism stresses the idea that I, as a reader, play a central role in determining meaning. Scholars such as Wolfgang Iser maintain that in the interaction between the reader and the text, "the role prescribed by the text will be stronger but the reader's own disposition will never disappear totally."[9] The reader's disposition will instead serve as a frame of reference for the act of understanding and comprehending the material of the text. Put simply, Iser takes seriously the identity of the reader when that reader reads any literary text. Thus, as a black Christian womanist biblical scholar who is troubled and angered by

---

8. See Townes, *Womanists Ethics and the Cultural Production of Evil* (Gordonsville, VA: Palgrave Macmillan, 2006), 12–27, particularly 12 and 24. The Aunt Jemima figure is an asexual southern motherly figure who opens up identity as property and commodity. The Sapphire figure explores anger in black women. The Tragic Mulatta is a mixed-race woman who embodies empire and empire-building through her overly sexualized nature. The Welfare Queen unpacks how religious values play a part in public policy formation, especially in relationship to the presidential campaign of Ronald Reagan; the Welfare Queen is also overly sexualized because of her willingness to have many children. The Topsy figure is a representation of a lazy slave girl who oftentimes needs to be whipped in order to get her to do her work.

9. Iser, *The Act of Reading: A Theory of Aesthetic Response* (Baltimore, MD: John Hopkins University Press, 1978), 37.

issues in contemporary society, the anger that sticks and swirls around me also sticks and swirls around my interpretations of the biblical text.

Engaging that anger takes me to the work of Sara Ahmed. Emotions, such as anger, circulate and shape social life. Theorizing that emotions generate effects that produce "surfaces," Ahmed finds that emotions involve the "sticking" of signs to bodies.[10] Drawing on such principles, Christian womanists must recognize the accumulative potential of anger, the ways in which the sticky substance of anger can generate meaning and engage communities in the work of justice. Anger is not irrational, as the dominant society suggests, but a catalyst that can build communities that in solidarity work for the betterment and liberation of one another.

Understanding anger in this way can provide a way to read the pain behind aggressive actions.[11] In the case of Newsome, I interpret the pain behind her angry action as a clarion call for continued movement against injustice. Womanist contextualization of identity in the midst of anger recognizes that anger becomes the form of "againstness" that allows us to move beyond the forms of injustice that occur in the world. As I think through womanist identity and the anger behind said identity, I propose the following hermeneutic as a way to read Herodias in Mark 6:17–19. My particular womanist hermeneutic is an interpretative method that takes seriously anger within womanist identity, thus allowing me to push back against traditional scholarship's characterization of Herodias and the anger that she embodies within the text. Accordingly, I now move to my reading of Herodias in Mark 6:17–29 and what it means for a womanist contextualization of identity.

MARK 6:17–29 FROM A WOMANIST PERSPECTIVE

Mark 6:17–29 tells the story of the imprisonment of John the Baptist by Herod. On the day of his birthday, Herod throws a party for himself and has Herodias's daughter dance for him and his guests. The Markan narrative states that Herod is so pleased with the dance that he promises to give the daughter anything she asks for. When she seeks her mother's advice, Herodias tells her to ask for the head of John the Baptist. Distressed, Herod grants the wish.

Naturally, according to traditional interpretations, Herodias and her daughter are to blame for the death of John the Baptist. I propose, however, that attention to emotions and context may unpack the Herodias story in ways that traditional scholars have not engaged or noticed.

The narrative states that Herod feared John, knowing him to be righteous and holy (6:20). I believe that this fear leaps to Herodias, thus making her angry

---

10. See Ahmed, *The Cultural Politics of Emotion* (New York, NY: Routledge, 2004).
11. Ibid., 173.

and allowing readers to see a clear manifestation of the stickiness of emotions. The transfer of emotions between Herodias and Herod creates a mood of helplessness wherein both Herod and Herodias are unable to communicate with one another. Accordingly, their communication occurs through an intermediary, Herodias's daughter. The daughter's body acts, in the words of Ahmed, as a surface on which the stickiness of both Herodias and Herod accumulates.

Given that Mark 6:17–29 is the only instance in either the Hebrew Bible or the New Testament in which one can read a conversation between a mother and daughter, I believe we must be especially attentive to the emotional stickiness that Herodias shares with her daughter and the unique relational dynamic involved. What are the contours of the violent anger that Herodias harbors within her body as a woman under the Roman imperial regime, and how does this violent anger affect her daughter and husband?[12] The Greek word *enecho*, which connotes an active sense of hostility or holding a grudge, at verse 18 provides a clue.[13]

Many interpreters note that, in a colloquial sense, Herodias had it in for John the Baptist. They interpret verse 19 concretely and without much additional thought—Herodias "had a grudge against him [John the Baptist] and wanted to kill him" (Mark 6:19 NRSV). But that interpretation does not adequately convey Herodias's experience as a woman within the unjust system of imperial society.[14] Given her identity within imperial society, I understand Herodias's unclear standing as a woman to be related to her anger: she has no control over her body nor her daughter's body. As a woman without control who lives in an oppressive system, she must take control when she can, thus, opposing the fear that her husband has evidenced within the text.

By tracing the impact of Herod's fear on Herodias's anger, I can begin to understand her actions differently. My reading, rather than blaming Herodias for her anger, allows me as a womanist reader to understand her anger. Herodias is a figure who holds violence within her body. The Markan narrative paints a picture of a woman who was easily moved from one man to another. Herodias, as with other women in the Roman imperial age, likely lacked agency in deciding whom she was to marry, as the easy transfer of women was one way men secured positions and privileges in the

---

12. Although I understand that René Girard's idea of mimetic violence has been influential for the study of Herodias and her daughter as mimetic counterparts, through a womanist contextualization of identity, I am attempting to read Herodias as a woman who has harbored violent anger within her body. Instead of focusing on the male leads in this story, I focus on the anger that Herodias must have experienced as a result of the limitations of womanhood within the Roman imperial period.

13. See H. G. Liddell and R. Scott, *Greek-English Lexicon*, 9th ed. (Oxford, UK: Oxford University Press, 1996), s.v. "ἐνέχω." Here, ἐνέχω connotes an active sense of having hostile feelings for or holding a grudge against someone.

14. See Joel Marcus, *Mark 1–8: A New Translation with Introduction and Commentary*, Anchor Bible (New York, NY: Doubleday, 2000), 395.

Roman imperial world.[15] How should a woman cope with being a piece of property that could be transferred from one man to another? How could a woman navigate such a world?

Moreover, Herodias was not able to secure a place for herself within this patriarchal society because she did not bear any sons.[16] Attentive interpreters of the text will consider that Herodias embodies an emotion of helplessness that is transformed into violent anger because her husband has the power to cast her aside. It is only through care, subtlety, and finesse that Herodias is able to accomplish anything during her time in the royal court. But John the Baptist seems ignorant of these realities, as he focuses only on matters of marital fidelity and seems inattentive to the canny skills required of Herodias if she is to navigate a dangerous environment.

Feminist biblical scholars have argued that both Herodias and her daughter have suffered violence at the hands of male scholars and commentators who read the Markan text.[17] One violent example interprets the actions of Herodias and her daughter as related to sexual depravity. Specifically, Frank Kermode brands both Herodias and her daughter as "cruel and sexually depraved." Dan Via, picking up on Kermode's language, argues that Herod's stepdaughter, a girl of about twelve years, is "apparently quite ready to exploit her charms publicly."[18] Such argumentation, which is accepted in traditional scholarship, evidences similar logic to a person concluding that a child appearing in pornographic literature has the ability and maturity to grant her consent.

Moreover, even some feminist scholars are complicit in misogynist language and interpretation when they identify Herodias and her daughter as inherently evil. For example, Susan Miller describes Herodias and her daughter as "evil counterparts" to the faithful women who follow Jesus as disciples.[19] The continued classification of these women as evil without contextualization is problematic. This assessment is unfair given the imperial context in which Herodias and her daughter acted, but it also has important ramifications for women outside of the biblical text. As our recent US elections have shown, many US citizens still have issues with women in politics, and this interpretation of Herodias may very well serve as an example to some conservative Christians of the dangerous consequences when a woman engages in the political arena—the beheading of righteous men.

15. Elisabeth Schüssler Fiorenza, *But She Said: Feminist Practices of Biblical Interpretation* (Boston, MA: Beacon Press, 1992), 48–49.

16. See Susan Miller, *Women in Mark's Gospel* (New York, NY: T&T Clark, 2004), 77.

17. Schüssler Fiorenza, *But She Said*, 48–49; Jennifer A. Glancy, "Unveiling Masculinity: The Construction of Gender in Mark 6:17–29," *Biblical* Interpretation 2, no. 1 (1994): 34–50.

18. Kermode, *The Genesis of Secrecy: On the Interpretation of Narrative* (Cambridge, MA: Harvard University Press, 1979), 130; and Via, *The Ethics of Mark's Gospel in the Middle of Time* (Philadelphia, PA: Fortress Press, 1985), 108.

19. Miller, *Women in Mark's Gospel* (New York, NY: T&T Clark International, 2004), 153–73.

Clearly, the historical circumstances facing Herodias and her daughter force them to make hard choices. During the imperial age, women were viewed as little more than passive objects or the prey of men's fancies. This insecurity is the catalyst for Herodias's anger and her desire to have John the Baptist beheaded. Rather than being unqualified acts of evil, their violence befits their violent context. As a result, their liberation required John the Baptist's execution.

CONTEXTUALIZING ANGER AND IDENTITY TODAY

Until the work of James Cone, much traditional theology failed to account for the nuances of identity. Cone argued that the gospel of Jesus Christ is the "revelation of God in Christ as the Liberator of the oppressed from social oppression and to political struggle."[20] If Cone is accurate in his assertion that the gospel of Jesus the Christ recognizes the political struggles and social oppressions of the disenfranchised, then the particularity of angry black women should not disassociate them from Christianity. Rather, it must be embraced as part of the black womanist Christian identity.[21]

Herodias displays angry emotions in the midst of violence and objectification. The contextualization of Herodias as angry, as a mother, and as a woman all point to the complexities inherent in identity. I am not advocating the beheading of a person as we read in the text, but I would advocate for the right of a woman to seek security in her marriage, to fight for the safety of her children, and to use her anger as a catalyst to fight against oppressive patriarchy and white supremacy. Accordingly, my anger as a black Christian womanist does not decrease or magically disappear because of my Christian identity. My anger remains, particularly when children are killed, when black men suffer mass incarceration at alarming rates, and when black women are abused for not fitting within the norms of a hegemonic society. No matter what, I can't stop the feelings.

---

20. Cone, *God of the Oppressed* (San Francisco, CA: HarperCollins, 1975), 81–82.

21. One womanist ethicist who embraces the duality of identity for black women well is Eboni Marshall Turman. Writing that the "church's understanding of Jesus is what informs its identity and propels its active articulation of that identity in the world," Turman then engages the Chalcedonian Definition to argue that God's ethical identity is predicated upon a womanist ethic of incarnation wherein black women possess both brokenness and the "coming-togetherness" of God's activity within their bodies. The both/and nature of Jesus and black women comes together in the multiplicity of black women's identities. See Turman, *Toward a Womanist Ethic of Incarnation: Black Bodies, the Black Church and the Council of Chalcedon* (New York, NY: Palgrave Macmillan, 2013).

20 What's So Holy about Matrimony? A Feminist Theological Reflection

by KIMBERLY HUMPHREY

"WHAT DO WE DO with this?"
Packing materials strewn around us, my fiancé and I stared at a beautiful glass pitcher that a friend had just gifted us for our wedding. It was elegantly engraved with the letter of my fiancé's surname. It was a surname that, in a few short weeks, neither of us would bear.

I had long held that I wouldn't change my name after marriage, and my fiancé, who felt strongly that he wanted to share a single last name, nonchalantly announced one day that he would take mine. With that casual statement, the patriarchal assumptions that I had long critiqued and attempted to hold at bay tumbled in: I felt guilty; I felt responsible; I felt like I needed to clean all this up and make things easier for everyone by relenting. Nevertheless, we agreed that he would take my name. We slowly started to come out about our future as the Humphreys.

All the while, I continued to feel on some warped, instinctual level that in this dimension of our life together I had already failed him. I had made his journey more difficult by refusing to take his name. I resented our culture for constructing the narrative that so pervasively argued that the role of a woman is to make a man's life easier, and I resented myself for buying it on this gut level.

Although many friends and family welcomed the news of my fiancé's name change happily (or, at least, quietly), others confirmed our fears by urging him to "be a man," even suggesting that this "show of power" on my part at the beginning of the marital relationship was a sure sign that I would eventually finish the "humiliation" by leaving him. We thought we had put the conversation to bed, but as we admired the mislabeled gift before us, it was apparent that we had not. Some months later, we still find ourselves engaging this subject with family, friends, and, occasionally, strangers.

Marriage remains fraught with social expectations and norms well beyond changing surnames. Our contemporary sociopolitical portrait of marriage is changing, but often it continues to be associated with overly simplistic renderings of security and stability. It is associated with tax breaks, with sexual stagnation, and with the boring and at times infuriating rhythm of day-to-day life. Much of our popular culture continues to use the marital relationship to represent our culturally expected settling, the transitional moments when hopes, dreams, and freedom give way to the demoralizing grind of office jobs and inspiration-sucking responsibilities. This narrative not only elides the true gift of commitment and friendship that marriage aspires to but it also strongly imposes cultural, economic, and political conventions onto our common imagining of marriage, conventions that often impede or misdirect embodied Christian discipleship.

To be sure, marriage can lead us to fruitful introspection—to find comfort in the arms of another who vows to love and care for us, who will be a refuge and a support. However, when the stability and confidence that comes with a healthy, supportive, caring relationship is conflated with the stability that comes as a reward for unthinkingly complying with sociopolitical and economic norms, it dangerously wears away at our impetus for engaging in radical critiques of social, political, and economic systems that disenfranchise vast swaths of the local and global population. This essay is an attempt to bring together the potential benefits of love and affection in committed romantic relationships with an interpretation of Christian discipleship that involves radical commitment to living the kingdom values of justice and mercy today. It envisions marriage as a locus of transgressive stability and stable transgression.

For my new husband and me, our faith and commitment to marriage find their fullness when they empower us to go out into the chaos of the world seeking and spreading God's justice and God's love. The feminist Christian reflections I offer here on marital identity are grounded in my most intimate relationships and concerns—this essay gets to the heart of the classic feminist proclamation that "the personal is political." I write it graced and burdened by the particularities of my body and context: I am a white, North American, Catholic, middle-class, feminist woman, and each of these factors informs my experience and understanding of marriage. It also must be said that our marriage is new, that we are young, and that we are exceptionally fortunate not to be directly affected by poverty, illness, or the broad denial of our basic human rights. Thus, while I seek a richer understanding of marital identity, I do not claim this marital identity as a definitive or universal goal; I merely intend to pose an alternative to the misguided norms and false promises that are often contained in our narratives of marriage.

SAYING "I DO" TO A FRAUGHT INSTITUTION

My own relationship to the institution of marriage is complicated by the fact that it has long trafficked in suffering and subjugation. Marriage has a history of misogyny as a tool of patriarchal control. It has been withheld from queer couples by both church and state. It has been manipulated and abused through white supremacist policies such as enslavement, mass incarceration, and merciless immigration policies that have violently interrupted the marriage and family relationships of black and brown Americans. And in our current era of the wedding industrial complex, the pathway to marriage and the re-formation of identity within it is often paved by economic systems of excess and exclusion.

In the Roman Catholic Church—my tradition—the two interpretations of marriage that have dominated in church teaching and culture have aligned with these sociopolitical and economic patterns. On one hand, marriage is associated with controlling sexual desire and activity. In this interpretation, married life is for those of us Christians who don't commit to the purer vocational path of celibacy. On the other hand, marriage is also held up as an uncomplicated domestic ideal that reflects the church's vision of gender complementarity.[1] Although this second vision is less suspicious of sexuality and sexual activity—at least in the form of vaginal sexual intercourse oriented toward conception—it continues to define the Christian marriage relationship in terms of classic feminine ideals (e.g., passivity, nurturing, and empathy) and masculine ideals (e.g., activity, providing, and protecting).

Throughout Christian history, members of the status quo have appealed to Scripture to support the sex-focused, highly gendered conception of marriage that we still see today in Catholicism. Within the writings of Paul, marriage is described as a conditional good, a committed legal agreement that places parameters around what was understood as the insurmountable temptation of sexual pleasure: "For it is better to marry than to be aflame with passion" (1 Cor. 7:9 NRSV). And yet even in this passage, we find the early Christian suspicion of marriage as a second-order choice for those who haven't lived up to the higher moral order of bodily asceticism:

---

1. Although gender complementarity has long been attributed to Scripture, contemporary constructions of gender in my Catholic denomination are largely indebted to the teachings of Pope John Paul II who delivered a series of "theology of the body" lectures in the late 1970s and early 1980s that were later published as an influential book. These lectures have little official authority, but their philosophical framework of gender and sexuality has become the standard for all official church teachings.

"I say this by way of concession, not of command. I wish that all were as I myself am. But each has a particular gift from God, one having one kind and another a different kind" (1 Cor. 7:6–7). In the same breath that this Pauline argument acknowledges married and celibate life as two different manifestations of divine gifts, it also posits married life as the morally inferior manifestation.

A few hundred years later, Gregory of Nyssa's "On Virginity" names sex and marriage as the root of suffering in mortal life. He notes that the ultimate goal of marriage is the pleasure of companionship but suggests that such pleasure is impossible given the marital frequency of anxiety, jealously, and grief. Moreover, he insists, the concerns of sex and marriage distract those involved from training their attention on God. Marriage, then, is a potential boundary to sacramental encounters, to recognizing God in our lives. The pursuit of a virginal life and an end to reproduction become signs of the kingdom whereas marriage and sexual activity are correlated with the fall, namely the distortion of the relationships between humans and God, other humans, and the rest of creation.[2]

John Chrysostom, a contemporary of Gregory, writes very differently of the role of marriage in a Christian society. In his words,

> The love of husband and wife is the force that welds society together. . . . Because when harmony prevails, the children are raised well, the household is kept in order, and neighbors, friends, and relatives praise the result. Great benefits, both for families' states, are thus produced. When it is otherwise however, everything is thrown into confusion and turned upside down.[3]

He goes on from this claim to defend Paul's infamous command for wives to be subject to their husbands, explaining that the relationship between husband and wife is parallel to the relationship between Christ and the church. Although Chrysostom cautions against the ill treatment of wives, claiming that no steady relationship is maintained through fear, he also claims that wives must "be subject in everything to their husbands, as to God."[4] In this way the church father propels the traditional narrative that men's existence more closely resembles God and that women are more damaged by the human capacity for sin. Although Chrystostom rejects violence within the marital relationship, he establishes quite clearly the (divine) lordship of the husband over the wife and this assumption of domination within the marriage.

Augustine's writings about marriage come only a few years later, but they differ in their focus, as Augustine was explicitly engaged in two prominent theological

---

2. Gregory of Nyssa, "On Virginity," in *Ascetical Works*, trans. Virginia Woods Callahan (Washington, DC: Catholic University of America Press, 1999), 13–14 and 46–47.

3. John Chrysostom, "Homily on Marriage," in *On Marriage and Family Life*, trans. Catharine P. Roth (Crestwood, NY: St. Vladimir's Seminary Press, 1986).

4. Ibid.

controversies. Against Manichaeism and extreme asceticism, Augustine defends marriage as proper to human experience—that is, intended by God before the fall. Against Pelagianism, he stresses the inevitable sinfulness of any sexual act and ties the good of sex—and by extension, the good of married life—almost exclusively to procreation. Along the way, Augustine loses track of the companionate view of marriage he had hesitantly developed elsewhere.[5]

Augustine's view of marriage, like Gregory of Nyssa's and John Chrysostom's, shows signs of two major themes in Christian thinking that remain influential to this day. The first is a Platonic tendency to separate the spiritual from the physical and to then subordinate the physical to the spiritual. We see this most clearly in Gregory's account of marriage, but despite avoiding the most extreme renderings of this dualism, Augustine also allows suspicion of the body and bodily desire to lurk in his writings. And the second long-lasting Augustinian theme is the sense within this framework that the spiritual and the physical were gendered: masculinity was associated with spirit and logic, and femininity was associated with bodies, materiality, and emotion. This continues the trend in Chrysostom's work of associating men with God while associating women with the church; women are the passive receptacle of God's activity and leadership. And with Augustine, marriage remains an object of suspicion—of fleshy temptation—even as society continues to ensure that it will be the primary identity marker and vocation for white women.[6]

This tendency, which celebrated the celibate male cleric as the closest thing to a perfect Christian vocation, reigned in Catholic Christian thinking until the Second Vatican Council. In the council's Dogmatic Constitution of the Church (*Lumen Gentium*) the first evidence of a new way of thinking about marriage and family emerged with an emphasis on the "domestic church":

> Christian spouses, in virtue of the sacrament of Matrimony, whereby they signify and partake of the mystery of that unity and fruitful love which exists between Christ and His Church, help each other to attain to holiness in their married life and in the rearing and education of their children. By reason of their state and rank in life they have their own special gift among the people of God. From the wedlock of Christians there comes the family, in which new citizens of human society are born, who by the grace of the Holy Spirit received in baptism are made children of God, thus perpetuating the people of

---

5. See Elizabeth Clark, "Augustine on Marriage," in *Feminism and Theology*, eds. Janet Martin Soskice and Diana Lipton (New York, NY: Oxford University Press, 2003), 245–57.

6. I use the word *white* here to recognize that in Western history, and particularly the history of the United States, women's confinement in marriage was primarily an experience of privileged white women. Women of color, especially African American women, were routinely forced to work outside the home because of unjust economic necessity. These circumstances were even more pronounced given how many African American men fell victim to white violence such as lynching, job discrimination, and mass incarceration.

> God through the centuries. The family is, so to speak, the domestic church. In it parents should, by their word and example, be the first preachers of the faith to their children; they should encourage them in the vocation which is proper to each of them, fostering with special care vocation to a sacred state.[7]

Although this shows a distinct shift in the ecclesial language about marriage and a break with earlier interpretations of marriage as a failsafe for the sexually weak, it continues to view the married couple only as a precursor to a nuclear family and not as a fundamental relationship outside of the parameters of children. There is beauty in the way the council merged the Scripture and the sacrament, and their motives in refashioning this doctrine seem appropriate, yet the image of marriage presented here is too perfect, perhaps tinged by the nostalgia of celibate men who have not fought with a partner about who last did the dishes or spent the wee hours of the morning cleaning up after a sick child. That is to say, although this passage takes family relationships seriously in the life of the church, the bishops missed an opportunity to truly reflect on the sacramental potential of marriage and family life as we experience it, with conflict and exhaustion as well as support, encouragement, and care.

Moreover, when we call marriage a "domestic church," it is easy to imagine family dynamics that mirror the hierarchal ordering that is so apparent in many Christian churches, particularly in the Roman Catholic Church. Within this framework, men/husbands/fathers rule over women/wives/mothers, and parents rule over children. This depiction easily brings to mind Chrysostom's interpretation of marriage as a relationship that relies upon women living as subordinates, in that it champions social harmony over just partnerships.

In the recent Apostolic Exhortation on the Family, *Amoris Laetitia*, Pope Francis recognizes Christianity's historical tendency to romanticize or generalize about marriage, writing that "At times we have also proposed a far too abstract and almost artificial theological ideal of marriage, far removed from the concrete situations and practical possibilities of real families. This excessive idealization, especially when we have failed to inspire trust in God's grace, has not helped to make marriage more desirable and attractive, but quite the opposite." Despite this awareness, the pope proposes perhaps the most idealistic model for marriage, one based on the inner workings of the triune God: "Seen this way, the couple's fruitful relationship becomes an image for understanding and describing the mystery of God himself, for in the Christian vision of the Trinity, God is contemplated as Father, Son and Spirit of love. The triune God is a communion of love, and the family is its living reflection."[8] Although there is nothing inherently wrong with orienting the marriage relationship toward an understanding of divine communion, it does not serve as a corrective to

---

7. *Lumen Gentium*, no. 8.
8. *Amoris Laetitia*, no. 36; no. 11.

the nostalgic idealism that Pope Francis laments about earlier ecclesial descriptions of marriage and family. In fact, Francis continues in the church's tradition of providing two extreme interpretations of marriage: as a second-class Christian vocation, the only alternative to which is celibate religious life, or as a reflection of the order and mission of God and the church, a view of familial and social stability that betrays the messiness of reality and champions the subjugation of women to men.

MARITAL STABILITY FOR DISRUPTIVE DISCIPLESHIP

Because both of these historical (and current!) conceptions of Christian marriage are seriously flawed, my husband and I were left wondering what might better encapsulate the gift and task of a marital partnership in the Christian tradition. Would it be possible to identify resources in the tradition and in contemporary scholarship that challenge these assumptions about marriage that pervade the religious and sociopolitical sphere in the United States?

As a newly married person, I've been disappointed at the lack of theological reflections on marriage that help couples navigate the major shift in identity from single to married and how this transition can positively affect how we understand ourselves as disciples in a world that is pervaded by distortions of justice and love. Pope Francis highlights these distortions in his writing about the damaging role of an inhumane economic system on the vast numbers of families who live in poverty, and he prioritizes such concerns in the life of the church as we strive to be a church of the poor.[9] In the context of that ecclesial aim, it is worth asking whether the marital relationship can be a locus of sacrament and discipleship, oriented toward the impossible task of living in solidarity with a people and a world in pain. That is to say, can marriage be holy?

This question points us to the sacramentality of marriage, a theological principle that can enrich our understanding of how marriage can shape and shift conceptions of discipleship and vice versa. To call marriage a sacrament is to claim that it brings participants into the intimate and immediate presence of God in a particular way. To be clear, I don't intend to speak of sacrament only in a legalistic, ritualistic sense but also to describe those mundane realities that make real the love of God to us. Rick Gaillardetz offers one image of the marriage as sacrament when he writes, "Marriage offers an opportunity to experience in a most intimate and sublime way the comfort

---

9. "In many ways, the present-day economic situation is keeping people from participating in society. Families, in particular, suffer from problems related to work, where young people have few possibilities and job offers are very selective and insecure. Workdays are long and oftentimes made more burdensome by extended periods away from home. This situation does not help family members to gather together or parents to be with their children in such a way as to nurture their relationships each day" (*Amoris Laetitia*, no. 44).

and solace in the arms of a spouse who commits himself or herself to use without condition."[10] This image of marriage—of unconditional presence to another in the face of crises big and small—is familiar and deceptively significant. We can catch glimpses of the seeming impossibility of God's love for creation in the willingness of another to say that we are good enough, despite all of our faults and failings and imperfections and despite the looming eventuality that we will one day lose each other.

Then marriage asks us to turn this sacramental encounter outward to the world—to be an active member of the local community, to participate in ministries about which we are passionate, to provide nourishment and care to our family, and to open ourselves and our relationship to be transformed by these practices. The experience of sacrament—an encounter with God's love—is an impetus to become a symbol of God's love to others. In a sermon on the Eucharist, Augustine famously says, "Become what you see, and receive what you are."[11] Although I have critically engaged Augustine elsewhere in this text, his contribution here is fundamental to Christian—particularly Catholic Christian—understandings of sacrament. Augustine's words tell us that in the Eucharist we not only receive the body of Christ but also become a part of it, empowered to live as Jesus did. The sacramental capacity of marriage offers the same challenge and hope.

That my spouse changed his name has become, for me, a perfect metaphor for marriage's capacity to be one form of sacramental discipleship. Although his decision was motivated, in some part, by a desire for stability and cohesion, it also challenged us both to rethink the standards for our relationship and our capacity to live differently—perhaps more justly—in a world that often sets up roadblocks to such change. I am sure that in the years to come, as we meet new people and form new relationships, most people will assume that our shared last name was originally his. In the end, this small protest, this radical yet hidden show of love, will be swallowed up by cultural norms. But the challenge of discipleship invites us to do much more as we consider the stakes of religious and civic involvement, community building, and the pursuit of justice and peace. We hope our defiant, common surname is only a small

---

10. Richard R. Gaillardetz, *A Daring Promise: A Spirituality of Christian Marriage* (New York, NY: Crossroad, 2002), 12.

11. Augustine of Hippo, "On the Day of Pentecost," in *Sermons*, vol. 7 of *The Works of Saint Augustine: A Translation for the 21st Century*, Sermons, trans. Edmund Hill (Hyde Park, NY: New City, 1993), 297–98.

and initial dimension of a long marriage that makes God's grace real in the world each and every day. Within the fraught history of marriage and within the messy entanglements that constitute particular marital relationships, we are challenged to subvert the marginalization that often resides in the status quo through sacrament, to grow the love shared within our relationship and send that love outward to God and all of creation with vulnerable hearts that long for justice. In this aspirational, experiential cycle, marriage becomes a paradoxical experience. The very relationship that promises stability and security also becomes a relationship that calls us out of cheap and easy comfort and into a life of radically uncomfortable and radically joyful discipleship.

21 Portrait with Eyes Turned Aside

by D. S. MARTIN

I've seen you look into a store window
the way I look into a book
like you   I begin   with what's inside
like you   distracted
when you find your image there
adjusting an errant strand of hair

Any word can form itself
                unbidden
into thought
or into a thousand pictures
any image   can be written back
into three-dimensional reality

A good window shows
what you already know
                encapsulates
the beauty of our self-conscious world
gives courage to change the things we can
though the wind blows   where it will

Contributors

Stephanie Berbec holds an MA in theology and culture from The Seattle School of Theology & Psychology. As an assistant theology editor at *The Other Journal*, she is particularly interested in thinkers who oscillate, sometimes profoundly, between theory and practice.

Derek Brown is a PhD student in systematic theology at Boston College. There, he is primarily interested in the relationship between theological aesthetics, liberation theology, and critical theories. This interest is the result of his undergraduate career in business, which taught him that capitalism is not good for the soul. While not at work, Derek is with his girlfriend, Deniz, and dog, Poca.

Judith Butler is Maxine Elliot Professor of Comparative Literature and Critical Theory at the University of California, Berkeley.

Lia Chavez is a New York–based multimedia artist whose work has been featured in the Venice Biennale, Istanbul Biennial, Armory Show, Tate, and elsewhere. Her work engages the nexus of art and neuroscience through installations, performance, painting, photography, and sculpture.

Zach Czaia is a poet living and working in Chicago, Illinois. His first collection of poems, *Saint Paul Lives Here (In Minnesota)*, in part a response to the clergy sex abuse crisis in his then-home diocese, was published in 2015 by Wipf and Stock.

Ryan Dueck lives in southern Alberta, Canada, with his wife, Naomi, and his twins, Claire and Nicholas. He blogs at *Rumblings*, and he is currently helping to lead a small Mennonite church that seeks to embody the peace, simplicity, and hope of the gospel of Christ in a noisy and conflicted culture. As all good Canadians must, he loves ice hockey, as well as soccer, books, good coffee, motorcycles, and mountains.

Julie M. Hamilton, a Baylor bear and Duke theology grad, is originally from central Texas and currently resides in Durham, North Carolina. Her creative hustle has ranged from galleries and nonprofit arts organizations to academic research, writing, and university development. She has been a staff writer for the *Curator Magazine* and has contributed to *Religions* and *SEEN*. She tamps espresso, adores baseball, and can usually be found watching films at the Carolina Theatre.

Peter Herman holds an MDiv from Union Theological Seminary in the City of New York and is a PhD candidate in theological and religious studies at Georgetown University. His work has previously appeared in the *Journal of Ecumenical Studies* and *Implicit Religion*. He spends a lot of time trying to balance the righteous outrage of liberation theologies with the peaceful reflection of Quaker spirituality.

Zen Hess currently resides in Greenville, South Carolina. He keeps busy working at a local bike shop, reading and writing, walking his dog, and traveling with Jessie, his wife. A graduate of Duke Divinity School, he writes regularly on the blog *Theology Forum*.

Kimberly Humphrey is a PhD student in systematic theology at Boston College and a graduate assistant at the Center for Teaching Excellence. Her work investigates the ways shame interrupts the capacity for Christians to remember dangerously and live justly, with a particular focus on the struggle for racial justice in a US Catholic Church that has been marked by white supremacy. She also supports and empowers survivors of sexual violence as a volunteer at the campus sexual assault crisis hotline. In her spare time, she enjoys cooking, hiking, touring breweries, and watching nineties sitcoms.

Katherine James has an MFA from Columbia University where she taught fiction and received the Felipe P. De Alba merit fellowship. She has work published in the anthology *In the Arms of Words* (2005), *St. Katherine Review*, and other journals. Excerpts from her novel, *Can You See Anything Now*, which was a semifinalist for the Doris Bakwin Prize, are in the anthology *Between Midnight and Dawn*, and one of her short stories was a finalist for a Narrative Spring Prize. A novel, as well as a memoir account of opiate addictions and overdoses in her community, is forthcoming from Paraclete Press.

Russell Johnson is a PhD candidate in philosophy and religion at the University of Chicago. He studies fear, disagreement, and why we talk past one another. His hobbies include volleyball and the culture war.

T. M. Lawson is a writer and poet living in Los Angeles, California. She has been published in *Los Angeles Review, Entropy,* and Poets.org, and she has forthcoming publications in the *Nomadic Journal, White Stag,* and *NILVX*. She is a 2015 Academy of American Poets prize winner and a 2016 Thompson Prize winner.

Sus Long is the frontwoman and songwriter for Hardworker, a rock band in Durham, North Carolina. Hardworker released their second album, *Go Alone*, in July 2017. Long is a musician, fiction writer, and poet, and she received her MDiv from Duke Divinity School.

D. S. Martin is a Canadian poet who edits the Poiema Poetry Series for Cascade Books. His books include *Poiema* and *Conspiracy of Light: Poems Inspired by the Legacy of C. S. Lewis*. He has also edited the new anthology *The Turning Aside: The Kingdom Poets Book of Contemporary Christian Poetry*.

Willow Mindich is a recent graduate from Colorado College, where she studied philosophy and psychoanalysis and founded *Anamnesis: The Colorado College Journal of Philosophy*. After a brief stint in Seattle, selling shoes, transcribing interviews, and teaching philosophy to fifth graders, Mindich has relocated to New York and is pursuing further questions of memory, culture, and technology while applying to graduate school.

Thomas Nail is an associate professor of philosophy at the University of Denver. He is the author of *Returning to Revolution: Deleuze, Guattari and Zapatismo* (2012), *The Figure of the Migrant* (2015), and *Theory of the Border* (2016). His work has appeared in *Angelaki, Theory and Event, Philosophy Today, Parrhesia, Deleuze Studies, Foucault Studies*, and elsewhere.

Oluwatomisin Oredein is a ThD candidate in theology and ethics at Duke University Divinity School. Her work focuses on Christian theology from an African diasporic perspective. Oredein is a contributing editor at *Marginalia LA Review of Books* and the author of the chapbook *i have stared down winters*.

Angela Parker is assistant professor of biblical studies at The Seattle School of Theology and Psychology. She received her PhD from Chicago Theological Seminary and her MTS from Duke Divinity School, and she is an ordained Baptist minister. She specializes in the Gospel of Mark, contemporary hermeneutics, womanist biblical interpretation, and postcolonial theory. When taking a break from teaching and research, she enjoys time spent with her husband, Victor, as they explore the Pacific Northwest.

Taylor Ross is a PhD student in the Graduate Program in Religion at Duke University. He writes at the intersections of patristic theology, theological aesthetics, and philosophy of language. He is also a member of the philosophy, arts, and literature graduate program.

Zachary Thomas Settle currently lives in Nashville, Tennessee, where he is a PhD student working in political theology in the Graduate Department of Religion at Vanderbilt. He is also the editor, alongside Taylor Worley, of a volume on theology, phenomenology, and film: *Dreams, Doubt, and Dread: The Spiritual in Film*.

Erick Sierra is an English professor who writes and speaks on issues of faith, society, and literature.

Jennifer Jane Simonton is a portrait and wedding photographer. After completing her master's in theological studies at Duke University in Durham, North Carolina, she moved to Minneapolis, Minnesota, where she loves slow mornings, witty humor, red wine, and tacos. She's infinitely curious, continually marveling at the magic of the everyday and that golden honey evening light.

Erin Steinke has had poems published in *Diagram*, *West Wind Review*, and other journals. After earning an MA in creative writing from the University of California, Davis, she relocated to Seattle and now teaches at Seattle Central College.

Pilar Timpane is a filmmaker, photographer, and writer. She is associate producer and editor of the award-winning oceanography documentary *Atlantic Crossing: A Robot's Daring Mission*, which premiered at the Smithsonian's Baird Auditorium in 2010 and aired on PBS stations around the country. She is also a producer of *Transforming Lives Media Archive*, a video archival collaboration between Writers House and the Institute for Women's Leadership at Rutgers University that provides young women with video mentorship and opportunities to make films about women in leadership. Timpane has lived in New Jersey, France, and Mexico but currently resides in Durham, North Carolina. The images included here were featured as part of our online feature "Identifying the Stranger: *Lamento con Alas* as a Means of Dignifying the Dead."

Mark Wyatt has been photographing people in cities around the world since around 1980, first on film and now digitally. He does not crop his photographs and processes them minimally, preferring to compose with the camera rather than with the computer. Wyatt posts new images regularly on his blog.

www.ingramcontent.com/pod-product-compliance
Lightning Source LLC
Chambersburg PA
CBHW081205170426
43197CB00018B/2926